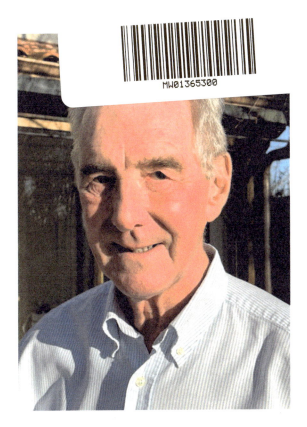

About the Author

James Hart is former Commissioner of Police for the City of London, having extensive operational and policy-making experience in British policing. He is co-author of 'Neighbourhood Policing', which has been nationally accepted as the preferred approach to policing and method of service delivery. He has experience of working in differing police cultures and environments, both in Europe and the United States. He holds a PhD in systems science.

The Future for the Thin Blue Line

James Hart

The Future for the Thin Blue Line

Olympia Publishers
London

www.olympiapublishers.com
OLYMPIA PAPERBACK EDITION

Copyright © James Hart 2023

The right of James Hart to be identified as author of
this work has been asserted in accordance with sections 77 and 78 of
the Copyright, Designs and Patents Act 1988.

All Rights Reserved

No reproduction, copy or transmission of this publication
may be made without written permission.
No paragraph of this publication may be reproduced,
copied or transmitted save with the written permission of the publisher,
or in accordance with the provisions
of the Copyright Act 1956 (as amended).

Any person who commits any unauthorised act in relation to
this publication may be liable to criminal
prosecution and civil claims for damage.

A CIP catalogue record for this title is
available from the British Library.

ISBN: 978-1-80074-974-0

This is a work of creative nonfiction. The events are portrayed to the
best of the author's memory. While all the stories in this book are true,
some names and identifying details have been changed to protect the
privacy of the people involved.

First Published in 2023

Olympia Publishers
Tallis House
2 Tallis Street
London
EC4Y 0AB

Printed in Great Britain

Acknowledgements

Neither my career or this book would have been possible without the support and encouragement of my wife, Julie, to whom I am hugely grateful.

Introduction

The Purpose of this book

The long established principles of British policing are in danger of being undermined by a range of threats that both individually and collectively have the potential to radically alter the widely respected style and professionalism of our policing services and the services available to the public. Some threats are new and have arisen from the criminal exploitation of the internet and misuse of social media, whilst others have been emerging over the past decade or so, such as a growing disrespect for some societal groups, the growth of Islamist terrorism, the significance of gang cultures, and the growth of international organised crime, including fraud in all its forms. These negative and unwelcome developments have the potential to disrupt the fundamental basis of a sound police service. British policing has been characterised by patrolling and preventing crime with tolerance and discretion, but the nature of the service is changing to a predominantly reactive style that has been exacerbated by severe resource constraints and poor decision making by governments of all complexions. This has left the police with little choice but to become more reactive with little time and opportunity remaining for more long-term preventive and reassurance strategies. Prevention is better than a cure!

It is not possible to draw a clear distinction between police, public, and political viewpoints on the topic of policing, as in the UK, police officers, police staff, and politicians are themselves members of the public. Mostly everyone, in all sectors of the community, has an opinion on their own levels of safety and security from crime, as well as those associated issues that negatively influence their quality of life. This book, however, is unashamedly written about policing from a police perspective; that is not to say it is supportive of everything about policing, or everything done by the police.

Clearly, it is right that both print and broadcast media highlight shortcomings in policing, but there are numerous pressure groups, think tanks, academics, politicians, lawyers, journalists, and many others who seem to be too hasty to both judge and comment on policing policies and practices without bothering to understand matters thoroughly. Policing seems to be a topic on which many have an opinion, some of which are better informed than others. This book therefore sets out to examine in some detail the UK policing principles and practices with an opinion that is hopefully well-grounded in evidence and pragmatism.

The future for policing is explored in a way that might enable contemporary decision makers to preserve the best of the established principles and practices, while at the same time preparing to tackle some very real threats. What it is not is an academic, or theory-based analysis. Neither is it a critique of former colleagues. It tries to illuminate some important contemporary issues that may be of interest to a casual reader who is curious to know more about policing services in the UK and some of the challenges faced by those delivering them.

The policing needs and expectations of the wider public, and of specific communities, change over time. Technologies and technological capabilities evolve, lifestyle choices alter, and crime trends similarly change. It is clearly necessary for the police to be sensitive to such changes and to recognise emerging trends. This means that police organisations need to be agile and well positioned to be responsive to the changes necessary to meet new challenges.

Some strategies for the future are suggested both for operational policing and for maximising effectiveness through organisational change. It is hoped that these proposals will stimulate interest in the topics and thus contribute to the discussion and development of policing into the twenty-first century. British policing has always been a global standard bearer and some might say a model of excellence. Whilst inevitably it is not always perfect all of the time, it does seem that there remains a great deal to be proud of. So, let's look to the future, '*Deep into the Blue*'.

1.

What is Policing?

What needs to be done

Most people, it seems, could have a stab at answering this one; it can't really be that difficult, can it? It also seems that this apparently simple question presents an irresistible opportunity for either over simplifying the nature of policing tasks, or, alternatively, providing a definition so mired in detailed analysis that the way forward is completely obscure, as might be observed in many police force 'strategic statements'. How officers and others are expected to understand, much less carry out, the duties implied by some of these glossy strategy tomes are a mystery. One thing is clear, though, and that is good policing is something done *with* people, not *to* people. In other words, policing in Britain, uniquely, is something done with the consent of the majority of the general public. The philosophy of 'policing by consent' implies that the principal party to the relationship is the public, not the police. It is they who allow police to exercise their powers. For instance, there is a general public acceptance of the fact that, in certain circumstances, police will arrest suspected offenders and, for a while at least, they will be deprived of their liberty. It is probable that a suspect would not agree with this point about consent, but it is seldom that the general public interferes with an arrest. Such is the nature of *how* policing is exercised in Britain, but this still does not get us closer to exactly what constitutes policing.

At its simplest, the principal role of police is the protection of life and property; but at the overly simplistic end of a scale of policing definitions, a senior politician once said something like, "...the job of police is to cut crime, no more, no less...". To make such a trivial remark is really to show a complete lack of understanding of what the majority of the public require of their police. The comment ignores all those police activities taking place twenty-four hours a day, three hundred and sixty-five days per year, which might generally be referred to as 'helping people'. Incidents such as dealing with emergency psychiatric cases, occasional unexpected child births, family and domestic disputes, missing persons, and many more similar calls from the public that do not necessarily involve crime or law enforcement. Indeed, it might be argued that to make such a remark is to invite the police and others to concentrate on the reported crime statistics that would illustrate the success of such a narrow policy. Of course, statistics are important to policing and this is a topic that is addressed in Chapter Seven, but to create a condition in which cutting crime is the only police activity is really a gross over simplification and an ignorance of the causes of crime. Conversely, if one were to draw up a list of the activities police officers undertake in their day-to-day work, it would make for tedious reading and be almost impossible to refine into a corporate strategy.

Arising from the undoubted diversity and complexity of the police role, over intellectualisation of policing has been very much a feature of the drive to appear rigorous in the analysis of policing problems. The result has often been some impressively glossy but impenetrable publications by the Home Office and, sad to say, some police forces. Such efforts at policing definitions would be at the opposite end of my scale and just as useless as the trivial catchphrase.

Therefore, in order to address the original question, it seems desirable to find a form of words that meets the needs of the public and the police by conveying, in a readily understood form, what police should do. After all, it's not much good having a policing strategy that is all embracing and which is completely un-memorable to officers delivering the service and, by extension, to the public also. Expressions such as 'the police are there to help society get on with itself', are insightful in a way, but not much help if one is striving for clarity in order to direct a large organisation. Similarly, lofty expressions about protecting life and property probably sound fine to the public, but, again, not much help in running a major, modern, public service confronted with determining priorities in the face of constrained or reducing resources.

It seems likely that an all-encapsulating definition of policing that satisfies both police and public will be illusive, desirable as it may be to have such clarity. Recent, and dare I say, fashionable attempts to sum up policing in a few words that can be fixed to the sides of patrol cars and incorporated into snazzy corporate logos also seem fairly useless, albeit well intentioned. What is one supposed to draw from expressions incorporating words such as 'protect', 'together', 'safety', and so on? Of course they represent aspirations for policing, but for police officers and staff, they often appear unrealistic, unachievable, wishy-washy, and nothing more than the product of an expensive senior management seminar. However, before consigning the notion of snappy mission statements, strap lines, and compact strategies to a policing wish list, it may be useful to examine the diversity of tasks that amount to contemporary policing, and as importantly, the public's expectations of contemporary policing.

Clearly, the public wants the police to arrive when they make a 'cry for help'. Response services are highly valued by the majority of citizens and indeed in the not too distant past, the function was considered so important that police forces were required to measure their response times to such calls and incidents. However, the statistics that measure police vehicle collisions didn't appear alongside those of police forces with the fastest response times!

The public also places a high value on crimes being detected by police. In fact, some would argue that the best form of crime prevention is a certainty of detection; perhaps a slightly flawed logic, but nevertheless indicative of the importance of catching the villains. Indeed, it is undeniably the case that relatively few criminals commit the vast majority of crimes of all types, so it makes perfect strategic sense to embrace crime detection policies that target the recidivist offenders. Indeed, recidivist offending is probably the phenomenon that gives rise to the most fear in the minds of victims and potential victims. For instance, the occurrence of domestic violence, in all its manifestations, is frequently committed by serial offenders who are either co-habiting with the victims, or who are well known to them and whose violent tendencies are well known. Sexual offences of all types are most frequently committed by individuals who have a history of such offending and, of course, such crimes are often associated with violence, which again tends to be a recurring feature of some criminals' behaviour. Whatever motivation criminologists and social observers assign to these crimes and the individuals who commit them, it remains a major function of the police to investigate and to bring reliable evidence forward with a view to prosecution.

As if the all-to-frequent reports of day-to-day crimes are not enough to deal with, the police have to direct significant assets to the investigation of 'specialist' crime. By this, it is meant those crimes that require specific and dedicated investigative skills and knowledge and frequently where the investigations are protracted by their very nature. Typical examples would be murder, rape, terrorism, serious fraud and other economic crimes, internet and 'e-crime' of all types, as well as some cases of abduction and organised crime, such as gambling fraud, immigration rackets, and illegal drug trafficking. Specialised activities such as the use of search teams, intelligence acquisition, as well as crime investigations, also extend to major public events, such as demonstrations, large scale disorder, and critical incidents of all types, including major sporting events. Some of the crimes arising from such incidents and events will clearly have an immediate impact on the victims, and the public at large, but often the impact on victims will be less direct and the effect more insidious. Senior investigating officers leading enquiries into such matters will be senior in rank and experience and have undergone specific training, not only in the subject matter of which they are specialists, but also in the leadership of such enquiries. This training will not only involve the legal and evidential aspects of investigations, but such topics as liaison with the media, cross (police) border issues, handling intelligence and forensic evidence, the administration and record keeping of the investigation, including disclosure issues, as well as resource and welfare matters. The training of such selected officers is thorough and time consuming but essential to meeting the needs of the criminal justice system, as well as the legitimate expectations of victims, victims' friends, relatives, and the wider public.

It is around this topic of serious and specialist crime, though, that some of the toughest decisions have to be made in relation to resourcing levels of particular investigations. It is very often the case that if such an investigation is given adequate resources at the outset, a conclusion will be reached much sooner than otherwise would be the case and this point is examined in more detail in Chapter Six. However, it is equally certain that it will not be too long before another serious and potentially unrelated crime will be reported that also requires the attention of the same specialists. Resources will have to be diverted to the new investigation, with the consequent frustration to all concerned with the previous matter. Making these decisions should be on the desks of chief officers of police (assistant chief constable, or commander in the City and Metropolitan Police) and such decisions frequently draw criticism from interested observers. The reality is that one cannot open another box of specialist investigators. Whilst neighbouring police forces, and those with requisite skills are invariably willing to supplement critical investigations, the requisite skills and resources are finite assets. It is worrying to observe how little attention is given to such decisions when various public and other enquiries are convened to determine why the police did not meet expectations in a particular matter. Suffice to say that the thorough investigation of serious and 'specialist' crime is a significant responsibility for the police (and serious crime agencies) and it is entirely reasonable that politicians and public alike have high expectations that satisfactory conclusions will be reached. One need looks no further than to some societies in other parts of the world, where organised crime and corruption has taken root, to appreciate the decaying affect such crime has on the quality of life. It is essential, therefore, that significant assets are dedicated to such matters. The creation (2012) of the UK National Crime Agency (NCA) as a development of the predecessor, Serious and Organised Crime Agency (SOCA), will make a major contribution in this regard.

Where possible, of course, preventing crime from occurring in the first place certainly seems to make good sense. Crime prevention as a function of policing is certainly important therefore, but as has been shown in recent times, the public and others can do much to help themselves in this regard, given some encouragement to do so. Police involvement in stimulating active crime prevention initiatives has been found to be almost essential if success is to be achieved in this regard. Property marking schemes, neighbourhood watch, with its many variants, and all so-called community crime prevention schemes invariably demand the police to initiate the action, with the hope that communities themselves will then take on the day-to-day operation of the schemes. There is no doubt that many such schemes have been successful and so too has the higher profile initiative of 'Crimestoppers'; a charitable organisation that collects anonymous information from the public on behalf of the police and, in some cases, offers rewards for information. Similarly, the popular television programme 'Crimewatch' has been most successful in attracting essential information from the public and raising the profile of particular crimes, often leading to their detection. Sadly, it seems decision makers at the BBC now no longer see this particular programme as attractive to viewers. The widespread deployment of CCTV systems in busy and crowded places has doubtless contributed to an improved quality of public life, as well as being an invaluable aid to investigations, and many local authorities have been very active in supporting such systems. However, despite the tremendous efforts and resources put into all these crime prevention ideas by non-police people, it is undeniably the case that the continuing prevention successes would simply not be deliverable without the committed and continuing involvement of police. So, it is not an exaggeration to say that crime prevention is a primary responsibility of police.

Dealing with anti-social behaviour has also been high on the political agenda in recent years, where many prevention initiatives have been less than successful. Although why some people blame the police and the failure of crime prevention schemes for the emergence of higher levels of street disorder is puzzling. What motivates young people, in particular, to become inebriated by alcohol and/or drugs and then behave in a completely outrageous fashion has surely more to do with parenting, or the lack of it, than the police, who have the unenviable task of dealing with such conduct.

The topic of anti-social behaviour in general was a major influence in the decision to create the post of the so-called 'Police Community Support Officers (PCSO's)'. The thinking, or what passed for it, was that more uniformed patrols on the streets would have a moderating influence on anti-social behaviour. I strongly suspect that the introduction of PCSO's (and I don't think I am alone here) was little more than a government cost-cutting exercise, as they are certainly cheaper than police constables. However, it seems that although there is a strong public desire for visible police patrolling, there is little political energy to pay for effective uniformed patrolling by qualified police officers, who have the necessary skills, training, and powers to tackle the problems seen by them and the public. This notion that visible patrolling is a desirable police activity seems to be contradicted by the fact that a very great deal of it is now carried out by PCSO's. If it is so desirable, and it seems that it is, then why is the function carried out by arguably the least skilled members of the police organisation? Surely, if the patrol function is a valuable activity, both in terms of providing reassurance as well as being on hand to deal with incidents, then it should be the principal activity of fully trained officers. There is, I suppose, at least one positive aspect to the use of PCSO's and it is that they are clearly the embodiment of citizens in uniform, which of course is a very strong constitutional element of the nature of policing in Britain and one that should be retained. Although this factor does not in itself justify the retention of PCSO's

There has been a good deal of academic research over the years to try to better understand the operational benefit, or otherwise, of the police patrol function. Many of the findings of these endeavours. by both the police themselves and various research institutes, have been contradictory, but the fact remains that most adults in the UK value the sight of patrolling police officers, preferably those on foot, wearing helmets as opposed to flat hats or baseball caps! So, it seems certain that, whatever else the police do, uniformed patrolling should constitute a major part of their work.

Uniformed response to major events is, of course, amongst the higher profile responsibilities that involve police in controlling and coordinating roles. A very senior colleague of mine once remarked that dealing with public disorder is the most difficult thing that police have to tackle. I don't think he was wrong, especially set in the context of major crime investigation, in which he was highly experienced. The public order/disorder management function varies from tackling small, spontaneous outbreaks of disorder, perhaps associated with low levels of violence, right through to major riots, where large numbers of people are injured, much property is damaged, and large numbers of police deployed. Such situations are almost impossible to control, and if indeed they were controlled to a point where the troublemakers were totally constrained, then undoubtedly the police would have to inflict significant violence themselves. This is often a tough decision point for police public order commanders, to weigh the costs in terms of injury to rioters against the other options, if any, for dispersal, containment, and/or intelligence gathering for later investigations leading to arrests. Such decisions are not straightforward, as is often suggested by interested observers, especially with hindsight. Complicated concepts of proportionality, reasonableness, the common (public) good, and the right to demonstrate are interesting and essential debating points in slow time, but are very difficult to rationalise and contextualise when extreme violence is occurring in a rapidly changing situation. Whether the individuals on the receiving end are protesters themselves, by-standers, or police, such situations can rapidly escalate in the level of violence and police commanders must be alert to the necessity to protect life. Despite which, it is also their responsibility to do their best to minimise the violence and disorder and to bring to justice those who are responsible.

Of course, there are shelves and computers full of police plans and operational orders for tackling public order problems, whether they are regular and pre-planned events, such as the Noting Hill Carnival in London, smaller scale celebrations, industrial disputes, major demonstrations, or spontaneous outbreaks of violence associated with revelry, sport, and alcohol. In all such matters, the pre-planning will specify the police strategy and provide tactical options to be deployed by ground-level commanders. All this will be signed off at senior level (customarily referred to as 'Gold') and carried out at ground level by 'Bronze' commanders, coordinated unsurprisingly by 'Silver'.

(The gold, silver, bronze command structure is the commonly used system for pre-planned event command and control. It is widely adopted by 'blue light' and other emergency services, as well as local authorities and those having to respond to potential major incidents, such as major chemical and oil installations. The most straightforward description is that gold sets the strategy for whatever event is anticipated, silver applies the strategy, co-ordinates resources, and is effectively the operational event commander, whilst bronze(s) are responsible for tactical command of individual functional units at operational levels)

It might not seem so from the front line of public disorder policing or other major incidents, but the toughest job by far is that of 'Gold'. The temptation on the day to involve oneself in the tactical command of a major event is almost unbearable, but giving in and micro managing the detail of the event is a recipe for turning a major incident into a major disaster. Always providing the ground level officers have been properly and thoroughly briefed prior to deployment, the very best leadership will allow the highly trained front line officers and their supervisors to get on with the job. Communications are never easy in public order situations, which are often very noisy. Despite modern radios, ear-pieces, and such like, changes to plans and the context for the changes will be extremely difficult to communicate in 'fast time'. Therefore, a change or variation to strategy during an event is very likely to cause widespread confusion and result in widespread dysfunction; hardly the best state of mind when facing extremely difficult public disorder challenges. It is not surprising, therefore, that public order policing is a clear specialisation and the officers involved at both command and front line levels are highly trained, with many having a very great deal of experience in dealing with such matters. The managerial challenge is, of course, to weigh the considerable resource commitments of sustaining the necessary level of expertise with the pressure to deploy experienced officers to other priorities.

This issue of specialisation versus generalisation, and the need to continually re-assess whether specialists are continuously and necessarily engaged with their discipline, is a topic that frequently recurs and one that will be visited in more detail in Chapter Six.

The skills associated with successful public order policing, particularly at command levels, are closely aligned with the necessary attributes for dealing with major and critical incidents, or other civil disasters. Central and local governments have varied and comprehensive plans for dealing with such incidents, which would typically involve significant, actual, or potential loss of human (or animal) life, major disruption to normal life and business, or any other event, natural or otherwise, that results in significant disruption. In the event of such an incident, it is the police who are principally responsible for coordinating and achieving the planning objectives, working closely with governments, other blue light services, and other responsible agencies. Even the 'lesser' major incidents are extremely resource intensive and often require police officers and others to work very long hours, frequently in conditions that are less than ideal. Where a major incident arises as a result of a crime or crimes, then the police role expands significantly in terms of both complexity and duration. Typically, such events would arise from acts of terrorism, major train or road collisions, aviation crashes, major fires, and similar incidents.

In the case of suspected sabotage, major incidents take on a particularly difficult complexion for the police as it is not always possible, or desirable, for the police to share their suspicions with a wider audience, including the media. And yet, if there is a crime to be investigated at the heart of a major incident, then it is clearly the responsibility of the police to obtain and preserve evidence. There is certainly best practice guidance available to the police in such circumstances, but this doesn't diminish the difficulty of combining a major crime enquiry with a conventional major incident response involving the prevention of further injury and tackling the aftermath of whatever it is that has occurred. The challenges for the police can be significant and, in some cases, highly traumatic for all those involved. Where there has been loss of life, one of the priorities will be accurate identification of the deceased and this is a function that requires close co-ordination between the scene, or scenes, of the event(s) and the hospital or mortuary, including the modes of transport between. The forensic recovery from the scene and from the deceased is a skilled and meticulous process that requires a thorough understanding of the potential evidential relevance of any particular sample. Such procedures can often be time consuming and delay a swift return to normality. Similarly, persons apparently missing from the scene of major incidents, major flooding for instance, is always a worry for police and skilled search teams are likely be deployed to undertake the explorations. Here again, search team operations and coordination is a specialisation and regular refresher training is a feature of this vital role.

Providing reassurance with relevant and timely information to a community overrun by a major incident is also a key feature of the police response, which involves the utilisation of other caring agencies and organisations. In many places, especially larger diverse communities, the police will already have well organised community liaison and involvement staff whose responsibilities on a day-to-day basis would include a knowledge of, and familiarisation with, community leaders and opinion formers. Such roles require sensitivity and patience from the police, as not everyone sees police as their friends and many tightly knit communities are suspicious of the motives of police. Nevertheless, community involvement and a knowledge of the priorities of local residents is an essential part of ensuring that policing takes place with the general consent of the law-abiding community. Of course, when some unforeseen disaster or major incident occurs, the ability to spontaneously engage with a particular community is a valuable asset. Therefore, it is important that as a part of routine police responsibilities, time and resources are directed to community engagement activities and projects. Schools, youth clubs, churches, residents' associations, clubs, neighbourhood watch, and community groups of all sorts provide an opportunity for the police to become closer to communities and be better able to understand their fears and priorities.

A vital feature of daily life that frequently brings people

into conflict, or disagreement, with the police is that of roads policing and traffic regulation enforcement. Whether it is dealing with collisions that result in injury or death, enforcement of drink and drug driving laws, or bringing prosecutions for speed or other driving regulations, invariably the person on the receiving end of the police attention will have an alternative account of whatever action the police have taken. Can there be any road user in the country that at some time or other hasn't moaned about police activity on the roads, or even the lack of it? Obviously, dealing with major collisions is a vital part of police work and here again, the skills necessary to accurately bring forward relevant evidence requires extensive training and re-training. Facilitating the movement of traffic after these events also places considerable pressure on police dealing with such matters. Both the real and opportunity costs of motorway and trunk road delays are massive and police are only too aware of the need to get things moving after a serious blockage, whatever the cause. Here again, forensic and other evidence recoveries are often at odds with the pressure to start traffic flowing.

In order to support this diverse range of operational functions and provide the necessary back office functions, police organisations are typically made up of sections and departments that support front line service delivery, such as intelligence and surveillance capabilities, forensic and high-tech crime units. Specialist patrol functions, such as mounted police, dogs, armed response capabilities, mobile support units, and public order specialists, are among the assets provided to support routine policing. Most specialist functions are made up of more experienced officers who are often trained to very precise and exacting standards, typically detectives, firearms officers, advanced response car drivers, and motor cyclists. Further support is provided to operational policing by what might be described as back office functions. Financial, human resource, facilities management, in fact just about every support function that would be found in any large, dispersed commercial organisation, but with the addition of those functions that deal directly with the criminal justice system, prosecutions departments, and similar.

Taken as a whole, police organisations are large (some are extremely large), multi-layered, complex, hierarchical, culturally rich organisations that support the delivery of a diverse range of services, twenty-four hours a day, three hundred and sixty-five days a year.

These functions and responsibilities, which have been broadly summarised, are what constitutes policing; additionally, there will be many specialisations that are sub sets of the principal policing disciplines. As will be appreciated, these tasks are largely complex and enormously diverse, making it extremely difficult to encapsulate in a meaningful mission statement and impossible to capture in a strap line!

Engagement with policing from both management and operational levels and from police and public perspectives would be so much easier if it were possible to answer the question, "What is policing?" in a straightforward, yet meaningful way. Commercial and many other public sector organisations have the opportunity to be quite clear about their purpose; to stay in business, to make a profit, to provide education, and so on. However, to summarise the British police function as simply protecting life and property, or reducing crime, is clearly some way short of what is generally expected by the public and indeed understood by most police officers.

Therefore, in the following chapters, some explanation will be given of policing activities, together with descriptions of the people and conditions that control the delivery of policing services. Some of the frailties and inefficiencies of contemporary policing are explored, together with some options for changes and improvements.

2.

The Police

Police are people too

"Who is a police person?" It has been previously noted that not everyone delivering policing services is necessarily a police officer. Police staff, or in other words those individuals working in police organisations that are not sworn police officers, provide an equally significant contribution to police organisations' efficiency and effectiveness. PCSO's are responsible for augmenting the front line patrol function, but are not police officers per se. However, the motivation and skills possessed by 'police people' will in many cases be similar, so it will perhaps be insightful to explore the necessary individual qualities that make up the personal characteristics of what has been called 'the police family'.

There has been much written about the unique status of the office of 'constable' in the context of UK territorial policing and the role is best described by the attestation, or oath, taken by constables on appointment as follows (There are minor variations for Northern Ireland, Scotland, and British Transport Police):

"I, ...of...do solemnly and sincerely declare and affirm that I will well and truly serve the King in the office of constable, with fairness, integrity, diligence and impartiality, upholding

fundamental human rights and according equal respect to all people; and that I will, to the best of my power, cause the peace to be kept and preserved and prevent all offences against people and property; and that while I continue to hold the said office I will to the best of my skill and knowledge discharge all the duties thereof faithfully according to law."

Essentially, the notion is that police officers are drawn from the public they serve, are apolitical, and reflect the priorities of the communities in which they work. This is a fairly sentimental view, however. Clearly, governments, and more recently 'Police and Crime Commissioners', will have priorities which to a greater or lesser extent reflect their political party's preferences, or their personal preferences if they stood as 'independent'. It is axiomatic therefore that these preferences will be reflected in the style and delivery of policing services; it would be naive to suppose otherwise. However, more importantly, when police make poor decisions, especially about priorities, it is often commented that the police only reflect the views and tolerances of the communities they engage with. This is a serious misunderstanding of the values that police must bring to their work. It must be the case that police people reflect the higher values of society and adhere to such values in both personal and professional life, as summarised in the above attestation. For instance, it certainly would not be correct for police to ignore racial offences because the community residents in which the events occurred were largely racists; if indeed such a community exists? Similarly, it would not be appropriate to ignore any other crime because the majority of a community supported the commission of that crime or its perpetrators.

Therefore, it should certainly go without saying that

personal integrity is by far and away the most desirable and essential characteristic of police people. Regrettably, however, it is a quality that is too often found lacking. There can be no doubt that the public impression of their quality of policing turns on the integrity of the police people with whom they come into contact, or about whom they are informed by the media. There can be nothing more disconcerting than to hear about, or experience, police falsehoods, whatever the motivation. Whether evidence is falsified for personal gain, or in pursuit of what is sometimes known as 'noble cause corruption'. This hopefully very rare practice occurs when evidence is falsified, exaggerated, or otherwise interfered with in order to secure a conviction, or to make a conviction more likely. Such corruption has most usually occurred when the police officer(s) is convinced a defendant is guilty, but where the evidence is considered to be insufficiently robust to be sure of a conviction. Similarly, and as corruptly, where an individual accepts some form of inducement, or bribe, to do, or not do, something that is manifestly their duty. So, in terms of personal qualities, it is imperative that police people possess the integrity to do the *right thing*, regardless of the pressures and temptations from whatever source to do otherwise.

That said, it is most important that police leaders recognise the pressures and strains that their people face in this regard. Starting at the very top, leaders should make adequate provision to safeguard their people from the attentions of corrupting criminals and others, who for whatever reason consider it advantageous to pervert the course of justice in its widest sense. It is undeniably the case that the British police are remarkably free of corrupt individuals within their midst, especially when compared to many other police organisations around the world.

This does not mean, however, that police chiefs should consider the problem to be so small as to not warrant serious and regular review. There is much that can be done, both in terms of policy and procedures that will not only prevent attempts at corruption, but will also reinforce the personal integrity of the great majority of police people who want to resist all such possibilities. Chapter Nine addresses some corruption prevention measures that regrettably should have wider adoption by police forces.

The roles performed by the majority of people working within a police organisation necessitates contact with communities to a greater or lesser extent. As by definition, and which has been noted, policing is something done *with* people, not *to* people. In terms of personal values, therefore, there is little to be gained by recruiting police people that have little or no affinity/empathy with others. If it were not in an individual's nature to want to help others, then there is little chance such a person would be successful in a police career. Helping people forms a large part of what police should do in terms of service delivery, and if this is not a characteristic that is naturally possessed by police recruits, then there is little chance of imbuing this through training.

This particular personal value, which might be defined simply as 'helping others', is of course closely allied to the concept of tolerance. Tolerance in its widest sense, of course, embraces community and individual diversity and includes ethnic, gender, sexual, and age-related issues. Police people not only have to be tolerant of such diversity, they also have to be sufficiently attuned to the needs of individuals and communities in order to anticipate the most appropriate way to deliver policing services. The failure, or inability, of police to grasp such a straightforward strategy will surely result in an inferior service being delivered. As noted earlier, the personal values associated with a tolerance for diversity, and preferably an active celebration of it, needs to be internalised by all police people. It is simply not good enough to turn up for work and make the right noises when others are listening, whilst privately harbouring inappropriate views. In order to adequately safeguard the rights and liberties of all individuals, police people must believe in the equal rights of all citizens and actively embrace their responsibility to protect this freedom. Victims, witnesses, and anyone else who has need of police services has the right and a legitimate expectation that this will be the case. So, favouring one community grouping, or their problems, at the cost of another is simply not a viable strategy for the delivery of long term, high quality policing services.

It is quite clear that in order for leaders of police organisations to be confident that the services they deliver are characterised by impartiality, then the police workforce needs to proportionately reflect the diversity of the population that is being policed, at least in terms of gender and ethnicity. Bold attempts have been made over the past two decades to moderate the predominance of white males in UK police forces and governments have even gone so far as to set targets for minority recruitment. Simply, each police force was given a target to achieve which represented the number of police officers within that organisation who should be from visible minority ethnic groups. Such initiatives stopped short, however, of allowing positive discrimination. Thus, police forces were deprived of the opportunity of favouring females and visible minority ethnic people as constables in preference to white males, when all other qualities and characteristics were equal. This short-sighted restriction has now proved to be very limiting to the development of a modern, tolerant culture within police forces and has caused regular negative comments that the police have far too few senior female, black, and Asian officers. The senior teams around the country's police forces remain constituted of principally of chief police officers[1] who are predominantly white males (Although it must be said that the recent Commissioner of the Metropolitan Police and the Director General of the National Crime Agency are both female since 2017). This lack of diversity cannot be appropriate or desirable in a country where differences are valued. There has been much debate about the difficulties females frequently encounter in reaching board level in commercial organisations, but it seems that even this is likely to be easier than reaching chief officer level in the police service. The only way to correct this situation is to make significant changes to recruitment practices and this subject is tackled later in this chapter.

To succeed in policing, individuals also need to possess high levels of personal motivation. Much police work is carried out individually and whilst, of course, working alongside colleagues is a highly valued activity, police people are often working on their own and thus need to have the drive to sustain what, on occasions, might be arduous tasks. Shift work, inclement weather, a demanding public, lack of physical fitness, reluctant witnesses, and abusive encounters can all conspire to dull motivation, and it is then that police people can fall back on reserves of personal motivation to see an investigation through.

---

[1] *The term 'chief officer' is used throughout to refer to a police officer of, or above, the rank of assistant chief constable in a provincial police organisation, or commander in the City of London and Metropolitan Police and 'civilian' police staff of equivalent ranks.*

It is perhaps when inquisitiveness starts to wane, whether through tiredness or any other reason, that a successful police officer will rely on his or her personal motivation to maintain curiosity. The result is undoubtedly satisfying, varied work, which is invariably highly valued and which can often be exciting as well.

Skills and skill levels are plainly topics that not only require a degree of application to acquire, but the training of them consumes a very great deal of a police organisation's resources, in terms of space, staff numbers, time, and equipment. Clearly, police people need to have the requisite intellectual ability to absorb and master skills training, whether this is in relation to basic training, legal and procedural matters, etc. or specialist skills requiring particular aptitudes. It is clear that if individuals were recruited to specialist support functions, such as financial and human resource management, then it would be necessary that they would be in possession of appropriate professional qualifications. There are also similar requirements for any other specific office function, such as secretarial, administrative, transport, building maintenance, and so on. But for police officers and, to some extent, PCSO's, it is really not necessary for individuals to have any particular qualification. The personal, empathetic qualities described earlier will, for the most part, be adequate to start with. It is simply not necessary to have, say, a law or criminology degree to be a good, effective police officer; it might help a great deal, but it is certainly not a pre-requisite. That is not to say that a good basic education is not necessary, clearly it is. Statements have to be written, oral evidence has to be given in court, reports have to be prepared. All of which require a good level of intellectual, written, and verbal reasoning. Verbal communication skills are clearly necessary and the ability to be easily understood is vital, but so too is the ability to listen and understand both spoken words and the nuances of speech. Much of this ability will accrue with experience, but it does underscore the importance of a diverse workforce, with police officers who are sensitive to the subtleties of communications within the communities they police.

As more experience is gained and leadership and management challenges start to form a greater part of the working day, then it becomes evident that those who have experienced higher education will tend towards successful selection for such posts. It has certainly been the case in the past that police organisations have invested a very great deal in providing access to higher education for those officers who have shown some potential for advancement. However, at present, with higher numbers of young people having first degrees and seeking employment in policing, the pressure has eased to provide higher education scholarships for suitable candidates from within. It has become, quite rightly, very difficult, if not impossible, to achieve more senior rank within the police service without evidence of some form of higher educational achievement. Indeed, much of the most valuable academic research that has influenced contemporary policing in recent years has been undertaken by serving police officers.

One of the most important features of policing in the UK is that police officers, or 'police constables' to give them their constitutionally correct title (regardless of rank), are officers appointed under the Crown, as implied by their attestation, and thus are individually responsible for their actions. This differs markedly from the situation in, say, the UK Civil Service, the military, and indeed in most overseas police organisations, where individuals are managed through a bureaucracy which ultimately accepts responsibility for the lawful actions of its members undertaken on the organisation's behalf. Clearly, all individuals are personally responsible for criminal acts they might commit. However, acts and decisions that are not criminal and are undertaken as a part of British police work are the responsibility of individual police officers.

So, for instance, it would be unlawful for a senior police officer to issue an order to arrest an individual; the decision to arrest is one for the arresting officer alone and it is he or she who is accountable by law for that action. In other words, the State does not protect an individual officer when acting on its behalf, as in other European countries, and neither does a police action become lawful merely because a senior officer says so. Clearly, there may well be case conferences where the timing of an arrest is discussed, but the ultimate legal responsibility is that of the arresting officer.

It might be argued, therefore, that the intellectual glue that binds these various personal attributes together is a personal robustness. That is not to say that police people should be stubborn, far from it, but it does mean that they must have the personal steadfastness to do what they know to be lawful and *right* in every situation. Being *right*, of course, is more than just being correct; it a matter of rationality based upon an understanding of the context of events, as well as individual actions. It is just as likely, therefore, that decisions made by a police officer will be *right* for some and *wrong* for others! Such is the nature of policing.

In comparison to other public sector workers, it is not surprising, therefore, that until recently police recruits were well paid (The starting pay for constables was reduced in 2013 by over four thousand pounds per annum). Police recruits are time consuming and difficult to select, expensive to train, expensive to equip, and because of this, important to retain.

It is these straightforward points that lead directly to some of the most controversial features of police recruitment and advancement that have mostly persisted since the formation of the British police service, that of the single point of entry. Until comparatively recently (2013), recruitment into the police service has been exclusively in the rank of constable, with the pay system almost exclusively linked to rank. In other words, everyone started at the most junior rank and worked their way from there to specialisations, higher rank, or both, with remuneration largely based on rank and experience, rather than skills, ability, and performance.

In order to populate differing police organisations with police officers with similar attributes, there is a national, standardised set of recruitment criteria for constables, which until very recently was the only entry point to a police career.

In 2013, the government introduced a system of direct entry to the superintendent rank, which is aimed at attracting high quality and experienced leaders from outside the police service into senior police posts after a rigorous eighteen month induction and training process. The system is clearly aimed at individuals with proven high achievement in other walks of life, and who display the abilities and attributes to reach chief officer rank in the police service. In a similar vein, in 2016 government introduced, through the College of Policing, a system of direct entry to the rank of inspector according to nationally set criteria. Indeed, other recent innovations in recruitment have allowed the police service to move away from the traditional single point of entry system.

Individual police forces will operate their own recruitment functions, but the training and testing of new recruits at all levels is to nationally specified criteria and standards, although it is the intention to include some locally set criteria in the case of direct entry superintendents, inspectors, and other fast track recruits.

The conventional recruitment system, whereby individuals join as constables, creates a pool of police constables who are broadly similar in knowledge and capability, working locally within their chosen police forces. It is generally from this strata of constables that officers study and train for promotion and/or specialisation and who then provide a resource for either the force in which they initially started, or from which other police forces might recruit. Such training is often provided locally, but more specialised training in, say, crime investigation, forensic recovery, or public disorder management may be provided on a regional basis, again to national standards. This approach to personal skills development and advancement has allowed a healthy transfer market between forces to develop. Police forces who want to attract the best talent and specialist skills by filling vacancies with skilled officers, usually on promotion, are invariably successful at attracting appropriate talent if an opportunity for promotion is attached to the post. The main problem arises, however, in that national pay scales prevent individual police forces from attracting specialists on a level rank transfer because they are only able to offer similar remuneration as the home force. In effect, this means that normally the only lateral movement, or level rank transfers, to take place are by officers who want to re-locate to another part of the country for either personal or professional reasons.

How much better it would be if police forces could

compete for the specialised talent that exists? The only reason they cannot do so is the stricture imposed by national pay scales. The benefits of moving away from this out-dated system and allowing individual police forces to set their own remuneration levels are obvious. Individuals would be more highly valued by their own forces, an incentive would be created for officers to tackle and succeed in specialist training, and successful applicants would improve their economic circumstances and bring diversity to their new employer's culture. Such a straightforward change to police pay regulations would have a marked impact on the availability of skilled officers to take on some of the more disturbing contemporary criminal activities that so trouble the public. As it stands, there is little incentive for police officers to take on such roles as they will attract the same remuneration whether they do so or not. There has been some attempt to remedy this situation by the payment of locally agreed allowances for particular types of work, but an allowance does not attract the same incentive as a salary increase. To continue with the present arrangement is, in organisational terms, simply not making the best use of existing resources.

This transfer market issue is closely linked to the existing, almost exclusively, single point of entry policy that has been a corner stone of police recruitment for generations. The thinking behind the policy is straightforward and is simply that police officers should understand and experience the characteristics of their work from the ground floor, or street level. Doubtless, there is much merit in this approach, both in policing and in other walks of life, especially when in the past individuals saw the police service as a lifetime career. It is also certain that credibility does attract to some individuals in more senior ranks as a result of this policy because the police workforce is aware that most senior officers have started out from the same position and have had similar experiences. Although, of course, it is generally not known with how much success. However, by continuing with this traditional approach, the police service as a whole is denying itself the opportunity to recruit available, well-motivated, and diverse talent. To some extent, this situation has been alleviated by the introduction of opportunities for direct entry superintendents and inspectors. Who after extended periods of both practical and classroom training are available for appointment to substantive positions in their rank, in just the same way as if they had progressed through the more traditional promotion system. In order to qualify for selection for these direct entry opportunities, the individuals must be of a very high calibre, physically, intellectually, and with high levels of social and communication skills. The necessary qualities are tested through a national assessment centre, which is a challenging experience for even the most able candidates. The problem, it seems, is that this process will produce a greater number of ambitious individuals who will almost certainly see their success in policing as being rewarded by further promotion. This begs the question as to whether there would be sufficient senior positions to meet the aspirations of these officers, or whether there will be a greater number of frustrated individuals who are unable to have opportunities that will meet their expectations. In any event, the point remains that it is individuals who possess particular skills for dealing with the demands of increasing and more detailed specialisations that are required. Such recruits should be attracted to policing as an opportunity to develop their specific skills and experience by lateral opportunities, rather than through engaging in the vertical competition for higher rank. It follows that a specialist who becomes 'super skilled' at some aspect of police work should also attract appropriate remuneration. In this way, skills and experience gained through concentration on specific topics would not be lost when an individual is promoted and usually moved on to some other aspect of police work or management. The point has already been made that the complexity of many aspects of modern police work require the dedicated application of individuals who have the knowledge, the networks, and the experience to be confident and successful in their work. There are many examples of where 'super-specialisation' is important and they span the entire spectrum of police activity. Fraud and cyber-crime, offences involving child victims of sexual crime, organised crime, including drug dealing, and people trafficking, major incident management, public disorder control, and the list could go on. It is simply not efficient to post officers to these types of functions for limited periods of time and then move them on to other duties. It is clear, however, that there are individuals who have considerable skill and experience in such matters who are not police officers, but who cannot be attracted into police organisations due to the restriction of the Police Regulations legislation, including the inflexibility of the pension arrangements.

It is clearly the case that individuals move occupations for many reasons, but it is equally clear that many would put themselves forward for police work if the opportunity existed for them to join at a point other than the bottom rung. This change, coupled with the opportunity to develop specialist skills or knowledge that they may already possess, would not only provide a more appropriate and experienced stream of police recruits, it would create stimulating work opportunities. As already noted, contemporary generations do not necessarily see a career for life as their desired lifestyle. Some preferring different occupations to suit different stages of their life, so second or even third career people may see the police as a desirable destination. However, such individuals, probably being older, are likely to have financial commitments that simply will not be satisfied by a constables' starting pay and so a policing opportunity would have to be ruled out. With the exception of the direct entry system for superintendents and inspectors, the police opportunity is simply not an option for them.

Similarly, individuals with specific skills or experience who want to develop their chosen interests might find the police a desirable development opportunity if they could be certain of being employed in a commensurate, or higher grade, than their current employment. It is possible that some such individuals would see the police as a longer term career opportunity, whilst others may see police experience as an enhancement to their *curriculum vitae* and be attracted by a short term contract. An obvious source of experience in this respect would come from individuals who have investigative experience in other fields, such as cyber-crime, commercial security, or from the plethora of other local and central government organisations that have an investigative or intelligence capability. However, similarly to those individuals who want to experience different careers, people from these sources are not going to consider a move if it is to their economic disadvantage. It seems there is no logical reason for a person who is to be employed by the police as, say, a child protection investigator should not come from a social services department, or an appropriate civil service post. It is likely that after suitable investigation training and some appreciation of legal matters, a well-motivated and knowledgeable investigator would develop with valuable non-police experience. As before, however, the police service is unlikely to be seen as an attractive destination if a transfer cannot take place on broadly similar, or improved terms and conditions, including transportable pension arrangements and related issues.

Specialist skills and knowledge such as these and others are desperately in demand by police forces. This need may be clearly illustrated by the ongoing controversy regarding rape investigations. Victims and their representative groups continually accuse the authorities, courts, and the police of not understanding the predicament of rape victims. The police repeatedly announce that lessons have been learned, procedures and training have been updated, and that things will improve. The reality, however, is that there are always competing priorities and without specialists who are broadly experienced across relevant agencies, dedicated to the investigation of such matters and the care of victims and witnesses, a lower than possible standard of service will be provided in this regard.

In short, the police service must encourage ministers to throw out these time expired, restrictive policies and implement recruitment practices that more closely follow commercial, market driven practices. It is only by these means that the police service nationally will be in a position to quickly and effectively respond to the public's ever shifting problems and priorities.

This situation raises two fundamental questions that will be addressed in relation to police people. Firstly, why is it necessary, or even desirable, for there to be restricted points of entry to the police? Secondly, and as already described, given the diversity of the nature of policing, why is a hierarchical rank system considered appropriate? (This topic is addressed in the following chapter, which concerns police structures).

The police ranks start with constable, progressing to sergeant, inspector, chief inspector, superintendent, and chief superintendent, then to 'chief officer' rank, which incorporates assistant, deputy, and chief constables, with slight title variations in London. Since the creation of the modern police in 1829 (save for exceptions concerning the appointment of Commissioners and Chief Constables pre-World War Two), all police officers join in the rank of constable, now including the two Commissioners in London and all Chief Constables. From this starting position, given ambition and success in both operational policing and examinations, individuals may rise through selection to higher ranks that are roughly based on a military model, with similar uniform insignia to that of the army. There are specialisations within each rank covering most of the topics described in the previous chapter regarding the role of policing. Most importantly, perhaps, is the distinction between those officers working in uniform and those engaged on other duties, such as crime investigation and associated work. Within this simplistic differentiation, however, there are many sub-sets and it is these 'super-specialisations' that present the major difficulty with a restricted points of entry recruitment system. For instance, there are few serious crimes involving fraud that do not require significant information and communication technology skills. Such skills are not exclusive to the police organisations and yet it is not possible to directly recruit such individuals as police officers and employ them within their specialisations. The less than ideal solution that is regularly adopted to cover such situations is that police staff, i.e. not police officers, are recruited to such work, or the necessary tasks are undertaken by consultants. That is not to say that either is in any way less satisfactory in their work, but that they generally have not been trained as investigators and do not necessarily have the personal values and attributes mentioned earlier. More importantly, perhaps, is the fact that they are not accountable as police officers and not subject to the police disciplinary procedures.

A situation is thus created whereby police organisations progressively become less and less flexible in the way that skilled resources can be deployed. If specialists are recruited, they tend to stay within their specialisation, whether or not there remains a need for their precise skills. Whereas if the individual were to be a police officer, they might be directed to another function of police work; lateral development in the HR jargon. Indeed, some would argue that to allow either police officers, or police staff, to remain in a specialisation for extended periods is to obscure from them the wider picture of policing, possibly resulting in a very limited appreciation of public needs. Consultants and temporary staff provide some opportunity to offer the best of both options, both with expertise and by not being a permanent drain on personnel budgets. The absence of the necessary personal qualities could, however, prove a liability in the longer term and, of course, the short term costs of such solutions is substantially greater, which can be problematic for annualised budgets.

So, what is stopping police organisations from recruiting the people they need, as opposed to a pool of generalists? Simply, 'The Police Regulations' grounded by primary legislation do not provide for recruitment outside specified national criteria, with specified national pay grades, pension, and conditions of service. It is simply not possible for individual police forces to draw up job descriptions for the specialists they need, with remuneration appropriate to a particular market, and then to set about recruitment. Small wonder that, when tackling some serious crimes for the first time, police officers are frequently left to learn things for themselves and to just get on with the job as best they can. A snapshot between a city police force and a more rural one can starkly illustrate this situation. A rural constabulary may well require individuals that understand farming and the agricultural sector, especially in the light of a trend to steal high value equipment, or to exploit an illegal immigrant labour market. A more urban police force may well require specialists in, say, a drugs market that is the front end of an organised crime syndicate, exploiting many aspects of human frailty and vulnerability. It is simply not efficient for such knowledge in either situation to be gained 'on the job'. Inevitably, and most desirably, experience will be a valuable attribute, but there seems to be no valid reason why police forces should not be able to recruit and train individuals with the necessary personal qualities to become police officers and who also exhibit the necessary specialist experience or knowledge to tackle some aspects of police work. This should be the case at whatever stage a person has reached in their chosen career or development. Why should it be assumed that a person generally joins the police during their younger years and remain in this pensionable position for thirty years or more? Many chief officers of police are appointed on fixed term contacts, so why not extend this opportunity to other ranks?

It is becoming increasingly apparent that many able people have the potential and desire for more than one career during their lives. A person might set out on one particular occupational course, but after a while decide, for whatever reason, that a change of direction is desirable. It seems negligent to the responsibilities of policing not to have provisions for making police recruitment attractive to such people. Flexible working conditions, flexible salaries, flexible and transferable pensions with flexible police attitudes to such recruitment, must become essential for contemporary policing to maintain quality and effectiveness.

It is, of course, acknowledged that such a raft of changes would not be without problems. The demands on an organisation making the transition from a tall, quasi-bureaucratic structure to a flatter, more 'organic' shape would be significant, but it is argued that the changes would be worthwhile both for police organisations as a whole and particularly for the individuals working in them. The outcome should be a far superior quality of public service, fewer mistakes, and improved public satisfaction. The topic of structures is tackled in the next chapter and a model for change management is proposed at Chapter Ten.

An obvious example of a rich pool of expertise for the police could be drawn from military sources. Indeed, there has been a steady stream of police recruits from military backgrounds since World War Two, but there is currently a huge disincentive for officers leaving military service during their mid-thirties in that they have to start again at either the lowest rank, or as a direct entry superintendent or inspector with a salary that can be easily exceeded in the private sector, where their experience is highly valued. The same is also true for many individuals who start out on a particular career, perhaps in a specific location, and after a while discover that neither is living up to expectations. The prospect of joining the police service would doubtlessly not be attractive to many such people, but there are certainly some to whom such an opportunity would be highly desirable. It seems, however, that many might be put off by starting at the bottom, or as a direct entry superintendent or inspector with the clear purpose of pursuing an upward career, as opposed to using acquired skills in a specific specialisation with a less than competitive salary and conditions.

Those who oppose such *radical* change do so largely from the position that, in order to understand policing, an individual must learn police 'street-craft' and investigations from the ground floor up. There is no doubt much to be said for this approach. It is straightforward, it does not require much imagination to understand, and it enables an administratively consistent approach to be taken towards recruitment and employment conditions; and lastly, it has worked, up to a point. Many of the most able police officers of all ranks would say that they learnt essential skills during their early years and from colleagues who took an interest in their development, thus sustaining the police culture. In contrast, a multi-point entry system would be difficult to administer and would probably not lend itself to a single, national system. Local recruitment procedures would have to be devised to suit local conditions, although it would be likely that, several years after implementation, best practices would probably become apparent. It is by no means inevitable, though, that colleagues who take great pride in developing skills in others would decline to do so because a new recruit had been appointed to an equivalent or even more senior grade to their own. The challenge would likely be to ensure that the organisational culture continued with the highest integrity, with high quality public service delivery at its core.

It was mentioned earlier in this chapter that there is an embarrassing shortage of females and members of visible minority ethnic groups within the police service as a whole and, in particular, within the more senior ranks. A part of this problem is the police service's reluctance, seemingly at all levels, to move away from the limited points of entry system. For all the reasons previously described, it is simply impossible at present for the police to recruit at any other level than constable, or direct entry superintendent or inspector. There is, therefore, little incentive for anyone, including females and members of visible minority ethnic groups, to even consider policing as a second career, or transferring later in life. It really is time that the police service and its staff associations recognised that to remain doggedly attached to such a limited points of entry system is just not sensible. To remain as at present will gradually attract ridicule of the police and it's leaders will be seen as stubborn, old fashioned, short sighted, and simply not up to the task of running major public sector organisations. This issue is of over-riding importance if the British police are to nurture their proud philosophy of policing by consent. There is now an enormous opportunity that would provide increases to the numbers of individuals from minority ethnic groups and females in the police service. It is quite clear that the police cannot attract sufficient numbers from these groups who want to sustain a full working life and a pensionable career, for many diverse reasons. However, what is equally clear is that as people age, they appreciate different values and priorities and are less challenged by what their peers or parents think about employment options. They are more inclined to follow career paths that they see as potentially satisfying. In a similar vein, there are many mature females who are content with their family and who are looking for something worthwhile on which they can exercise their skills and experience. It just does not make any sort of management sense for the police to retain out dated recruitment policies that exclude and discourage such people.

It seems that despite the historical merit of the single point of entry system, the current arguments do not acknowledge the significant advantages that could be drawn from radically changing the current arrangements to a multi-point entry system. It is undeniably the case that policing is becoming more diverse and more complicated. More and more specialists must replace the traditionally trained generalists if effectiveness is to be improved upon. The simplest way of achieving this would be to open the police recruitment process to a wider pool of interested and talented individuals. Such applicants could be drawn not only by the prospect of interesting and worthwhile work, but also by competitive conditions that reflect contemporary private sector practices.

It seems that the role of the police staff associations, The Police Federation (representing ranks from constable to chief inspector), and the Police Superintendents Association have made no secret of the fact that they prefer national pay and conditions for their members and this would naturally correspond to a national rank structure. The Home Office similarly and doubtlessly preferred a system that was administratively similar across the country. This made control of the police, principally through financing, a much more straightforward task. Indeed, there was an attempt by the Home Office to allocate resources through a funding formula, on the grounds that a similar police activity and a similar person in one part of the country should cost the same as in another. In a similar vein, a recent proposal from the Home Office (which was not taken up) was to create 'strategic police forces' that would essentially be of similar numerical size, regardless of the nature and features of the communities that were recipients of their services. What were seen as the operational benefits of this proposal are obscure at the very least. Quite why Home Office Ministers, the Civil Service, and others who advise them thought these were good ideas remains a mystery; suffice to say that police force boundaries remain unchanged and the funding allocated to the newly appointed Police and Crime Commissioners will be on a different basis. The examples do, however, illustrate the Whitehall obsession with creating a standardised and administratively similar policing landscape.

As with other larger public sector, service delivery organisations, police forces have a mixture of employment cultures. Police officers who fit into a clearly defined rank structure are generally well paid and cannot strike. They work alongside police staff who do not necessarily comply with any of the police strictures and, as a result, different working cultures develop. The vast majority of problems that might be anticipated to emerge from such an arrangement are trivial and are overcome by good sense and a desire to deliver a good service. It must be noted, however, that this is not always the case. In the worst manifestations of culture clash, police officers can be deliberately antagonistic towards police staff, who then become obstructive and dilatory. The result of which is that service quality drops as more time and effort is put into fighting internal turf wars than into delivering outcomes. This issue of clashing cultures is not trivial and can account for many negative practices that harm the efficiency of a police organisation and contribute to resistance to change.

Should the necessary alterations be made to enable the police to embrace a multi-point of entry recruitment system, leaders will need to be alert to the potential problems faced by newcomers to the police who occupy senior posts. For instance, in many police forces, individuals cling to formal titles and require these titles to be used in everyday language, such as 'sir' when subordinates address inspectors and above, with sergeants being addressed by their rank title. Other less formal terms of address are common and vary from force to force, but typically 'boss', 'guv', 'sarge', 'skip', and similar are part of everyday policing vocabulary. A person entering the police who has been used to, say, a first name culture, or being called 'mister' or 'miss', etc. would find the verbal culture very strange indeed, especially if that person was more mature and had experience of styles of address in other organisations. In this context, as well as in respect of other organisational cultural matters, it would be important to avoid alienating existing, established police officers and staff by undermining their perceived status. It is also clearly evident in any well led organisation that individuals hold their leaders in high regard and this respect for authority often manifests in the terms of address used, for instance calling someone 'mister', 'missus', 'doctor', 'chairman', etc. as a term of respect. It should not be overlooked that it is important to many people to have their relationship defined by a term of address with their colleagues, which also provides a known structure where relationships are clear. Again, perhaps it is now time for the police to re-think some of these cultural issues, such as terms of address, which undeniably reinforce the rigid, hierarchical, and formal authority level structure of many, if not all police forces, and which contributes to a damaging lack of flexibility.

There are small scale, limited training opportunities for officers seeking to join neighbourhood policing teams where first name use is the norm. So, in theory at least, there is no compelling reason for maintaining the current main organisational title practices

It is apparent that if police forces are to be successful in addressing the tasks set out in Chapter One with energy, professionalism, and the highest integrity, then recruitment policy and methods have to change. Suitable police people have to be recruited from diverse backgrounds, ages, and experiences in order to attract the skills necessary to continue to meet the evolving challenges faced by police forces. The attractiveness of the improved effectiveness that could be drawn from alterations to these features is irresistible in the current climate.

3.

Police Structures and Governance

Who is in charge?

Having suggested that there are critical issues to address in order to develop the best of policing, those of the rank structure and the limited points of entry offered by the recruitment system, this chapter will propose models of organisation and structure that have the potential to improve some aspects of the current operational performance. Before doing so, however, it will be useful to review some current features of organisation and structure that will have a bearing on future designs.

Essentially, there are forty-three territorial police forces in England, Wales, and Northern Ireland, excluding the Channel Islands and the Isle of Man. The structure is loosely based on county boundaries, but with some groupings and boundary variations that reflect local circumstances and needs. Each police force (the term 'force' is used as synonymous with the term 'service' that is preferred by some) has its own Chief Constable, or Commissioner in the case of the City and Metropolitan areas of London. Each police force has its own headquarters, with central functions and common services in much the same style as many private sector head offices. Front line, or day-to-day operational policing, is delivered through territorial Basic Command Units, each usually headed by a chief superintendent, or superintendent, who is accountable both to the public locally and to his or her chief constable for performance and budget disbursement. The chief constable in turn is accountable to the 'Police and Crime Commissioner (PCC)' who is locally elected for the policing area concerned, and who will agree policing priorities and overall budgets. The appointment of these individual PCC's is a relatively new initiative (2012) and it remains to be seen how effective they will be in replacing the function of the former police authorities.

Generally, each police force will have a range of specialists available to deal with special types of crime and disorder, or in some places regional facilities to which they have access. These police officers, with their back office support, will be located at police headquarters, or a headquarters satellite location, and work under the direction of senior officers located centrally and who are without territorial responsibilities. Typically, a police force will have groups of officers specifically trained to deal with public disorder, searching, maritime/riparian work, and other specialisms, depending upon local need, and various departments and smaller units who specialise in investigating particular types of crime. Child protection, domestic violence, rape, murder, vice, and drugs are typical examples, but the list will be longer and more diverse in larger police areas and embrace such topics as counter terrorism, fraud, and internet crime. Traffic, or roads policing, and the response to an investigation of serious collisions, as well as other major incidents, are also functions carried out by all police forces. Although a great deal of the response capability to motorway incidents is now undertaken by the Highways Agency employees, freeing up highly trained police officers for other response duties.

Of some significance is the wide range of police force sizes, as measured by police numbers, residential populations, business population, visitor numbers, and geographic area. Naturally, the larger urban conurbations have the highest number of police officers serving larger populations than in less built up areas, where police officer numbers are proportionally lower. Similarly, the more rural police forces cover much larger areas, but with proportionally fewer officers, serving a smaller and more dispersed population. This significant variation in size has been the subject of much debate over decades of policing evolution and, from time to time, amalgamations have been made to create larger and potentially more efficient police forces. A major effort by the government during 2005-6 to significantly alter the policing landscape by a series of amalgamations failed on the basis that the resulting organisations would be unlikely to reflect local conditions and priorities. Further, that larger and more remote police organisations would not be seen as having sufficient local accountability. Sensibly, the government withdrew these proposals and the patchwork of large and small police forces remains for the foreseeable future. However, the eight Scottish police forces amalgamated into one organisation on the first of April 2013; whether this move signals a direction for Wales, or indeed England, in the future remains to be seen. However, it does seem as though the Scottish experience has not delivered all the anticipated benefits of amalgamation. Rather, the urban/rural contrast has exacerbated the effects of centralisation, amongst other things, and leant weight to the benefits of local policing suited to a particular environment.

One of the major influencing factors in the police amalgamations issue is the question of the public's cultural identity, or what people understand to be their area and mental map. For instance, residents in Devon, Cornwall, Dorset, and Avon & Somerset identify broadly with the region of the South-West. Similar regions can be envisaged covering other grouping of cities, towns, and counties around England and Wales. The problem with attempts to rationalise boundaries in the past seems to have been that scant regard has been paid to such cultural identities, thus exacerbating the feelings of being policed by some unaccountable, remote bureaucracy that is administratively and numerically consistent, but has little recognition for the public's identity. An approach that denies the significance of cultural identity really runs counter to the principal of policing by consent.

Localism is an important issue which will be discussed later in terms of police accountability and a future model, but suffice to say that reflecting local circumstances and conditions in the size and shape of a district police force is a fundamentally important feature of British policing. At the other extreme of this debate, would be a national police force, remote from the communities it purports to serve and governed by individuals geographically remote from the area of service delivery, raising many questions of accountability, identification of priorities, and performance. So, despite the apparent anachronism of the smallest police forces having less than a thousand officers and the largest over thirty thousand, there is very sound sense to having police forces that reflect local conditions and not giving way to enthusiasm for an administratively elegant and economic landscape of similar sized organisations.

The demands on police change over time, however, sometimes slowly, sometimes less so. For instance, there is no doubting the negative effect of the criminal exploitation of the internet that has significantly altered the nature of many incidents to which the police have to respond. The grooming of young people for sexual exploitation, the recruitment of others to become drug dealers across police boundaries, national and international fraud, and the importation of illegal migrants are all recent developments to which the police have to find solutions. This place a much greater emphasis on the need for internet and other data specialists, which has implications for the size of police forces; clearly such investigators have to be drawn from somewhere. Simply, the small size of many police forces will limit the ability to provide the necessary specialists in sufficient numbers. A solution may be to regionalise these types of capability, but problems would then doubtless arise from the prioritisation of cases and the urgency that could be applied to critical incidents, although examples exist where serious crimes, including murder investigations, are successfully investigated on a regional basis. A regionalisation approach may well be the solution to providing adequate specialist services that is short of creating a national police force, with all the attendant accountability and governance problems. A possible model to address these issues is proposed in Chapter Eleven.

The Neighbourhood Policing[2] initiative, implemented in trial form in the Metropolitan and Surrey Police areas from 1982 onwards, identified a number of critical issues for police to adopt in order to maintain the local focus and accountability that was argued to be essential. If the Neighbourhood Policing provisions were to be implemented in their entirety, then there is certainly a case to argue that the sizes of police forces should

---

[2] *Neighbourhood Policing (1981) James Hart & Ian Beckett, The City University, London.*

be more consistent. There is a credible case that such a change would at minimum be more economic in terms of the number and size of headquarters units and, by extension, the numbers of senior (chief) officers. For the time being at least, however, it seems that the locally focused police force structure, with its local accountability through PCC's, will remain.

Until very recently (late 2012), chief constables and their police forces were held to account for both performance and budget disbursement by police authorities. These police authorities constituted local government councillors, independent members, and magistrates. Generally, they met once a month or so and received reports on a range of both operational and administrative matters, including details of complaints against the police, either in full meetings, or sub-committees. Generally, these arrangements worked well and it was plainly to the surprise of many police authority members and police officers that the government preferred a system of individually elected PCC's in 2012. This new system, by offering party political candidates for election to the post, manifestly brings the opportunity of direct political influence to the function of local policing that hitherto had remained apolitical.

The appointment of PCC's was controversial and many senior police officers were privately most concerned to see the police service being subject to political control in this way. It has been noted that it is somewhat naïve to believe that policing can be separated from politics, in so far as it is a costly public service and, as such, must be amenable to government policy. However, to re-introduce a direct political overseer at individual police force level is to return to the pre-1994 period when former police committees reflected the political colour of their county council, or metropolitan authority. This situation was seen as undesirable and the system of police authorities was introduced, which is discussed in more detail in Chapter Four.

So, as far as governance is concerned, the significant issue is that a PCC has the power to appoint or dismiss a chief constable. In respect of appointing a chief constable, it is interesting to observe that many of the individuals appointed as PCC's have little or no experience in senior appointment selection procedures and it is apparent that some, at least, see this selection process as a personal responsibility, rather than one to be shared with others. As far as dismissing a chief constable is concerned, again PCC's appear to have taken this heavy responsibility as a personal power and not one to be shared, so it seems that personal relationships will play as large a part in such considerations as professional competence, or the lack of it. There have been several high profiles, public disagreements between a few chief constables and their PCC's that have been well publicised. These events have not created a good image for the PCC system. To the contrary, many media reports have portrayed the PCC's concerned as being too impatient and lacking judgement by jumping to conclusions. Time will tell whether these relationships settle down to a business-like arrangement, or whether other decisions will be formed after clashes of political opinion between the PCC's and their chief constables.

Whilst the national structure of policing is an important issue, and accepting that, to some extent, structure will be an element in determining policing style and the quality of service delivery, it is the people within police forces that are the key resource. It is the structure and organisational relationships of these police people that is more critical to the style of service delivery and to effectiveness than police force size and boundaries.

It has already been mentioned that a component of the transferable skills problem is the anachronistic police rank structure. Whatever the reasons for its implementation and evolution to its current form, it certainly does not meet the needs of a modern police force. In brief, it is too tall, too top heavy, and the rank titles don't give any clue as to role, with some titles bordering on the absurd. For instance, what role is implied by the rank of 'deputy assistant commissioner'? If this isn't bad enough, salary is mostly linked to rank and most pay bands are butt-ended, so that once an individual has reached the top pay point in any one rank, the only option to increase his or her remuneration is to compete for promotion. There are a few minor allowances paid for special skills, but these have a negligible impact on the overall approach to remuneration. Here again, this produces a de-skilling affect as it is likely that if an individual is working in a specialist role, then promotion will lead to a move away from that function and into another role at the higher rank. The result of this process is that the upper echelons of police forces are invariably made up of generalists. This may not be a bad thing for the most senior (chief) officers, but for those charged with responsibility for specific types of activity, for instance counter terrorism, murder, fraud investigation, public dis-order management, and such like, it is a negative factor and a great disadvantage. Skills, experience, networks, and knowledge are lost to the function because many individuals, quite understandably, have ambitions to improve their personal economic position.

This point conveniently leads to addressing the question which concerns the organisation of police people; that of the hierarchical rank structure of police organisations. As noted earlier, the rank structure is quasi-military, as in the tall, triangular shape of police organisational charts and in the appearance of uniform insignia, with progression through one rank being a prerequisite for advancement to the next. It is not clear when this rank structure was introduced, but it is likely that as early chief constables were largely senior, retired military officers, the ranks owe much to their influence. The established rank structure has seen off a few minor amendments during the last several decades, but it remains essentially rooted in the classic, bureaucratic, hierarchical model, which gives greater legitimacy to decision making the higher the rank of the decision maker. All the problems associated with tall structures may be found in police organisations. Poor and slow communications from the top, with poor and slow feedback from the bottom. A frequently encountered lack of respect for the competence of more senior people by the more junior. A willingness to pass decisions upwards with a general difficulty in locating the origin of specific decisions. Clearly not everyone, everything, and everywhere suffers these problems acutely, but in terms of organisations' characteristics, the hierarchy constrains good practice in these respects.

It would also be true to note that the current rank structure has, to a large extent, dictated the shape and internal boundaries of police divisions, or basic command units. Essentially, areas of police territory within individual police forces have been determined by the police numbers required to deliver a standard service rather than by any other factors. So, a simple example for instance; it may be determined that a chief superintendent's span of command would involve a workforce of, say, eight hundred officers and police staff. Therefore, in an urban area, police density would be concentrated. Whereas in a more rural area, the concentration would obviously be far less, creating both a physical and knowledge distance between police and communities and making the leadership role correspondingly more difficult. The management structure and the number of more senior officers thus being derived from the front-line numbers. The result is administratively similar management structures across the country that has more to do with securing comparatively equivalent responsibilities through numbers than providing a structure that reflects local issues, complexities, and features. With limited pay flexibility and pay points within each rank, the only significant way, therefore, for a police officer to increase remuneration is to achieve higher rank. This means that specialists who want to remain as such are generally denied the opportunity to develop upwards, except perhaps in the largest police organisations.

The rank structure may therefore be argued to be one of the major limitations on the progressive development of police organisations. In truth, there is little that Chief Constables and Commissioners can do to remedy this situation. The role of certain ranks is specified in several major pieces of primary legislation and to implement changes peremptorily would be to fly in the face of established law, which could amount to an illegal act in itself. For instance, the decision making role of superintendents is quite clear in relation to several provisions of the Police and Criminal Evidence Act, as is the role of assistant and deputy chief constables in relation to provisions within the Regulation of Investigatory Procedures Act. So, in order to alter the police rank system, it would be necessary to amend associated primary legislation and this obviously requires government energy.

The problems do not end there, however; it may also be argued that the rank structure has been responsible for significantly constraining the way in which the UK policing style has evolved over recent decades. Policing in the 1960's was a very much tighter regulated activity than today. There was a good deal of active front line supervision, applied with a strong disciplinary style of leadership, supported and encouraged by invisible senior officers who generally expected to be treated with great deference. The result was almost certainly a generation of police officers who treated the public outside the police stations in much the same way as they were treated inside. It is not unreasonable to suggest, therefore, that many of the high-profile policing problems of the 1970's and 1980's might be tracked back to this inculcated, authoritarian style of front line policing, which was not appreciated by all sections of communities. However, to the very great credit of generations of officers following, this style has largely been replaced with a much more empathetic and participative style of leadership, but this has been achieved despite the rank structure, which steadfastly remains.

A change from a hierarchy of ranks to a system of grades, with appropriate and descriptive job titles, would give much greater opportunity to reward specialist skills, rather than time serving and seniority, as at present. Such changes would also facilitate both the introduction of a multi-point entry system, together with an appropriate remuneration policy, as described earlier; some suggestions on this topic are offered in the next chapter.

It is likely that there is no single reason for not altering the rank structure, or at least giving individual police forces more flexibility in how they organise themselves. The first issue to tackle should therefore be to reduce the 'height' of the rank structure by simply reducing the number of ranks. This was attempted during the early 1990's, but subsequently the situation has gradually reverted to the previous arrangements. Associated with the height problem is one of 'top-heaviness', so it makes sense to examine both issues together.

Promotion to both sergeant and inspector necessitates the passing of examinations through an assessment centre process in practical, procedural, and legal matters, which is often then followed by a further interview selection process. Sergeants perform a front-line supervisory role, whether they are investigators, other specialists, or meeting patrol and response requirements. Their contribution to on-the-job training, quality control, and adherence to procedures is vital, therefore the rank should remain, but perhaps the titles should change. At minimum, the terms 'patrol supervisor' or 'investigations supervisor' would convey to the public something understandable and meaningful about the role.

The rank of inspector is often perceived as the first step towards more senior rank, but because the work undertaken by inspectors is so varied across police forces, it is not possible to make a generalisation about the exact role of this rank. What is clear, however, is that the vast majority of inspectors are managers of something. They allocate resources to problems, are accountable for results, and often take on more serious and complex investigations requiring a depth of experience. There is meaning in the job title up to a point, in that inspectors 'inspect', amongst other things. However, what is more confusing is what constitutes a chief inspector's role; more of the same actually. It would therefore make perfect sense to combine both rank titles and significantly extend the top pay point of an inspectors' salary to the current top point of a chief inspectors' salary. Provided the top point of such a scale could only be achieved by appraisal and selection, rather than time-serving. Considerable incentive would be provided for advancement. Similarly, as discussed in Chapter Two, an immediate opportunity would be created to recruit people into the police service in an established rank with a long salary scale. The point here, as already argued, is that the nature of advancement is lateral, encouraging specialisation and expertise in a specific role, rather than the only advancement being promotion in rank

Moving up the ranks to superintendents; recent attempts were made to abandon the title of chief superintendent and combine both levels with a single rank of superintendent divided into two grades. This change quickly slipped back to the previous arrangement, simply because chief superintendents are always in charge of a fairly large portion of a police force and it is as well that everyone knows who is in charge by virtue of title. However, the notion that the two ranks are confusing to onlookers is sound and it would make perfect sense to have a single rank, but differentiate a more junior grade. The term 'director' is widely used in both public and private sector organisations and accurately defines both the perception and reality of what is involved in a chief superintendents' role. It would be logical, therefore, to allocate the rank title of director to chief superintendents and assistant director to superintendents. As with the proposal for inspectors, the pay ranges should be extended and progression through pay points should be by appraisal and selection rather than time-serving. Here again, a great incentive is provided to potential transferees from other organisations, as well as ambitious internal candidates.

Achieving the promotion from the rank of chief superintendent (or exceptionally superintendent) to chief officer level has typically been amongst the toughest selection processes in the public sector. Candidates for appointment as assistant chief constables (or commanders in London), firstly have to be supported and graded in their application by their individual forces for appearance at a national assessment centre, where intellect, aptitude, and experience are probed. Success leads to further grading and the opportunity to attend a course, or series of courses, designed to equip successful candidates to manage police forces at the highest levels. The grading that is assigned at the conclusion of this process is highly significant to future promotion selection. Competition is quite rightly intense and the failure rate is correspondingly high. Despite the rigour of this process, it does seem to favour those who are able to submit to the programme of courses, which necessitates absences from both home and work, which of course does not suit everyone's lifestyle. It is possible, therefore, that there is built in bias within this process that needlessly discriminates against some sections of the police; females for instance.

Given personal success and the support of the Home Office, these chief superintendents are qualified to apply for advertised posts as assistant chief constables around the country, or as commanders in the London forces. Generally speaking, it is necessary at this level for successful promotion aspirants to move between police forces, often leading to the need to re-locate or commute on a weekly or longer basis. The policy has its exceptions, however, and the vague rules have been frequently re-interpreted to allow a particular officer to remain in his or her current force. Similarly, it is generally not possible to be an assistant, deputy, and chief constable (or equivalent) in the same police force. However, exceptions are made and whilst the original rules were well intentioned as an anti-corruption measure, it does seem as though such measures have run their course and that post holders should be the best candidate for the post, rather than having shortlists constrained by previous appointments. Successful appointees as assistant chief constable or commander leads to the opportunity to become a deputy chief constable, deputy assistant commissioner in the London Metropolitan Police, and onwards to assistant commissioner, chief constable, and commissioner. A seriously top heavy structure, where differentiation between rank and role becomes nearly impossible to define.

So, despite the fact that the archaic rank structure of UK policing is at the root of a number of significant organisation problems for police, there has still not been a serious initiative to tackle the issue. Indeed, if the matter is not urgently tackled, the current problems caused by the structure will escalate and doubtless others will emerge. That said, as previously noted, in 2012, Her Majesty's Chief Inspector of Constabulary[3] (HMCIC) did produce a report that made a range of recommendations that were accepted by the Home Office concerning police pay. It does seem, however, that this was a missed opportunity to radically change internal structures, rationalise ranks, grades, and remuneration in order to create police organisations fit for the twenty-first century. The problems outlined in this and the previous chapter will not be resolved to the satisfaction of potential police recruits, existing police officers, and the public they serve unless the conditions that have created the current organisational problems are completely altered; tinkering

---

[3] *Winsor Report HMCIC 2012*

around the issues is not a solution. Whether or not more radical reform was resisted by staff associations or others is not clear, but what is apparent is that more needs to be done to tackle some of the issues described.

This situation leads to another characteristic of police leadership that would benefit from change. It will be clear that all top police officers have experienced a similar development path. Rigorous as this might be, it does mean that, by and large, chief officers have similar outlooks and experience. Obviously this is beneficial when it comes to commanding police operations, but it is likely to be a constraint when leading a multi-disciplinary team, managing a multi-million-pound budget. Some progress has been made towards tackling this problem and senior members of police staff are encouraged to experience the chief officers' training programmes, which effectively place them on equivalent grades to their police officer colleagues. The problem as has been shown previously, however, is that the process is not open to candidates from outside the police service and therefore inhibits diversity in the top police ranks. If a particular police force wants to engage, say, a new director of finance, then advertisements would be made and a process put in place for selection. Having appointed the most suitable candidate though, there would be no guarantee that such a person could experience chief officer training, or indeed experience a wider role in the governance of the organisation, rather than being restricted to only the finance portfolio, for instance. Development in such a role would be entirely dependent on the views and assessment of the chief constable. In effect, this means that the police service is missing out on experienced, high achieving, senior leaders from other walks of life who might have the ability to bring much freshness to police force management. Such people are unlikely to leave their current roles given the uncertainty of their sphere of influence and the constraints applied to remuneration.

To tackle some of these matters, it would seem sensible firstly to rationalise some of the job titles attached to chief officer ranks. There is no discernible reason why the London forces should refer to their first chief officer rank as commander and for provincial forces to use the title assistant chief constable; it would surely make sense to call everyone in this rank 'commander', as that is precisely what they do. The situation in the provincial forces with regard to deputy chief constables is equally vexing. In the recent past, a dreadful muddle was created when the 'rank' of deputy chief constable was abolished and substituted with an assistant chief constable, who became the 'designated deputy'. Everyone inside and outside the police service was confused and succession plans for some officers' careers suffered as a result. Unless an assistant chief constable was a 'designated deputy' chief constable, he or she would not be short listed for chief constable selection. So, where an individual was working in a police force where there was already an established deputy chief constable, there was no opportunity to move upwards and no more deputy chief constable vacancies were advertised; the result was stagnation from a policy that had not been fully thought through.

Rather than open these controversies again, it is suggested that the rank of deputy chief constable remains, principally because it describes the occupation of the post holder. The situation in London is, however, not at all straightforward. Chief Constables are called commissioners in the London City and Metropolitan forces, with assistant commissioners judged to have equivalent rank to chief constables in the provinces. The real problem for the public understanding comes with the rank title of deputy assistant commissioner (DAC), which is exclusive to the Metropolitan Police and roughly equivalent to that of a deputy chief constable in the provinces. Following the logic of previous arguments, it would be entirely reasonable to combine the rank of commander with that of DAC, extend the pay scale upwards to the current maximum for a DAC, and allow applicants to compete for moving to higher pay bands on the basis of appraisal and selection, rather than time-serving. So far as the job title of 'commissioner' is concerned, it seems unlikely that either the Metropolitan or City Police would easily relinquish these titles in favour of 'chief constable'. Despite the logic of doing so and the confusion created by the government's creation of the title 'police and crime commissioner', who are entirely different, elected appointees. It would seem tolerable to retain these titles as they are specific to London and really not an issue elsewhere.

These proposals are straightforward enough and would certainly do away with much of the public confusion about who does what in policing. As importantly, however, it would break down the out-of-date views in some parts of the police service that progression can only be made through time-serving and upward movement through a jumble of ranks, the principal feature of which is to specify pay grades. Most importantly, however, the problems of encouraging and rewarding specialisation would be addressed and the police service as a whole would be opened up to staff markets and greater diversity in its leaders.

The beneficial side-effects are also worthy of mention. A contrast has already been made between the police officer culture and that of police staff. As noted, whilst this is not typically dysfunctional, these alterations to the police rank structure, and the way in which remuneration is assigned to roles, would bring police employment conditions closer to that of police staff, who's arrangements are more akin to that of the Civil Service and local government employees.

It has long been accepted in larger commercial organisations that significant value might be added to boardroom deliberations by the contributions of suitably qualified non-executive directors (NEDs). In policing, no such opportunity exists and even the presence of police staff functional specialists as members of the top police team does not bring the breadth and insight that NED's might contribute. This problem would be lessened, however, if police top teams (chief officer level individuals) could be directly recruited from outside the police service. To some extent, this problem of non-police involvement was not a difficulty when police authorities existed, as it was always possible for police leaders to take soundings and advice from individual police authority members who displayed the necessary independence of thought. However, given the latest arrangements with the appointment of PCC's, it is difficult to appreciate from where a police top team might draw reliable counsel. The solution need not be one or the other, NED or full time external appointment, but rather a combination of both. It seems that some PCC's have recognised the omission of external and independent contributions and have set about recruiting 'advisors' who, it is assumed, will be able to provide relevant advice. However, as with all advisors and consultants, understanding the nature of the problems to be tackled is a major factor, as is locating the ownership of the problem. To some extent, this difficulty can be overcome by a

NED who has regular and unrestricted access to the leadership of the police force and who will accumulate knowledge on his or her own behalf over a longer period of time.

Implementation of these proposals would inevitably require at least a measure of co-operation from the police staff associations, who are potentially the strongest resistors of change in this regard (See Chapter Ten). It will be clear, though, that the proposed alterations to the rank structure completely negate the distinction between the Police Federation (ranks to chief inspector) and the Superintendents Association. Onlookers may find it difficult to understand why these two separate staff associations should exist; indeed many serving officers would find the distinction difficult to explain. Historically, a distinction has been made between the pay and conditions of ranks up to chief inspector and the superintending ranks. For instance, overtime compensation can be paid to the federated ranks, whilst superintending ranks are salaried for twenty-four hour responsibility.

The solution is straightforward; merge these the two bodies, thus simplifying negotiations with the police workforce as a whole and, at the same time, providing police officers with harmonious representation that is not fractured by arbitrary rank divisions.

As far as chief officers are concerned, it is clear that, until quite recently, there was much room for improvement both in terms of the roles of the former Association of Chief Police Officers (ACPO) as a staff association and that of its policy role. At the core of this problem was that ACPO attempted to represent the senior leadership of the police service in every respect. It endeavoured to provide representation in respect of pay and conditions in much the same manner as any other professional body. It sought to influence government policy through the various business area groups and sub committees. It sought to harmonise police procedures and policies that benefit from national compliance. It organised conferences, seminars, and exhibitions and. in theory at least, provided the Home Office ministers with a point of contact with the police service as a whole. However, in terms of governance, ACPO was dependent upon the willing compliance of chief constables to abide by its agreements and decisions through the council of chief constables. There were not any mandatory elements within ACPO processes, however, and from time to time individual chief constables would decline to follow the majority for their own local reasons. This led to difficulties in the ACPO leadership delivering a common outcome on behalf of the police service as a whole. In short, the arrangements were a mess and doubtless most unsatisfactory to government and others. Recent decisions have separated the staff association functions of ACPO and the policy function, which has been assigned to a development of the former chief constable's council, now known as the National Police Chiefs Council (NPCC). Efforts here are made on behalf of the forty-three territorial forces and are closely linked to the work of The College of Policing, who develop common policies and standards. Various 'lead officers' from around the country's top teams take on the development of specific policy areas and provide public facing opinions on a range of specific topics, as well as providing advice to government and others.

Despite what some would claim to be an unnecessarily complicated representation arrangement for police and policing, it would be highly desirable if chief officers could lead the necessary revisionist work and changes with the Police

Federation and Superintendents Association. It is certainly the case that, in the future, police forces need to have staff recruitment and selection policies and procedures in place that more closely reflect practices in the private sector, where top quality staff is the principal organisational resource. The problem is that the people who write the rules are generally constrained by what has gone before and do not have the experience, or the vision, to break from established practices, despite the perceived intellectual benefits. There is not a safe route for these changes; change will be difficult and demanding on all those involved (Chapter Ten) but the need to grasp the opportunity is clear. Failure to do so will leave the police moribund and a victim of enforced change, which would be undoubtedly the worst outcome.

4.

Police Accountability

Who is Responsible?

The accountability of police officers and police forces, and who holds them to account, are topics that have exercised the minds of politicians, sections of the public. and the police themselves since the inception of professional policing. Police accountability, as an all-embracing concept, consists of the systems and procedures, both formal and informal, through which the police are bound to give open account of their actions and decisions and which gives practicality to the philosophy of 'policing by consent'. Such systems and procedures are diverse in character and embrace political, legal, personal, and ethical issues, at both local and national levels. In recent times, the subject was brought to prominence during the aftermath of inner city riots during the early 1980's and has subsequently never been far from high profile. In order to explore the various factors relevant to police accountability, it will be useful to briefly review the various accountability arrangements that have been in place since that time.

    The 1980's riots in London and elsewhere were trigger events, in so far as they exposed what had been a simmering discontent of policing in many areas that eventually boiled over into riots around the country. The assortment of enquiries that followed highlighted the depth and extent of the gulf that had developed between the residents of some inner city areas and the police themselves. In very simple terms, the police perceived that large numbers of people, largely from minority ethnic groups inhabiting congested urban areas, were responsible for much of the crime and disorder. Conversely, many of these mainly younger people saw the police as racist and overbearing. Given the social circumstances of that time, it is quite likely that such attitudes towards the police were not confined to inner cities but extended across the country with varying degrees of intensity. Generally speaking, it does seem as though there was an increasing distrust of the police brought about by, amongst other things, a weak police complaints system, an authoritarian police attitude towards public disorder, a steady stream of reports of police corruption and wrong-doing, coupled with a generally 'closed', almost secret, style of operation. The public was very unclear about what drove the determination of police priorities and, indeed, how it was decided what was done and what wasn't.

Local police committees of the time (as opposed to 'police authorities) comprised of local councillors and magistrates, and were the principal means by which provincial chief constables were, in theory, held to account. In reality, many such police committees had little more than token effect on police operations and were seen by many police chiefs as an unnecessary encumbrance and hindrance to their management and status. Police committees were typically organised and operated by county councils, who provided the necessary support and administration as well as more specialised services of financial and facilities management. Indeed, most police committees were run very much along the lines of any other county council committee, where the chairman was elected by committee members. In the case of larger provincial police forces spanning several local government areas, police committees were of a similar style and function, but representative membership was drawn from regions and magistrates courts covered by the police force.

In the jargon of the time, the so-called 'tri-partite arrangement' was the means by which police forces were controlled. The three parties being the local police committee, the Home Office, and the chief constable in person. The system being that the chief constable had operational control and independence in that regard, but was accountable in other respects to the police committee. The central government, or Home Office, influence was exercised through the office of the 'Inspectorate of Constabulary' who periodically checked up on police force performance and conformity to Home Office directives. In the case of London, the role of the police committee was exercised by the Home Secretary in person, the public accountability being through Parliament itself. Whilst in the City of London, a fully elected committee of the Corporation of London operated along similar lines to other police committees. With the exception of the City of London, it might be argued that the governance of policing at this time was largely obscure and distant from public involvement. It is perhaps not surprising, therefore, that the issue of accountability became a hot topic after the 1980's riots.

In order to overcome these well-founded views of police isolation from their communities, local consultation groups were formed that took a variety of forms around the country, but essentially provided a forum at which local police commanders could be questioned publicly about police activities and priorities. This scheme also provided an opportunity for the police to consult with the public about their views and concerns. In various forms, such groups still exist. But since the statutory formation of the so-called 'police authorities' in the 1990's, community consultation became and remains a much more formalised process.

Police Authorities differed from the former police committees in that they were independent from local governments and administered themselves through a full time executive team. Thus they were effectively separated from the political influence of their former local county and municipal councils. They were, however, constituted of local counsellors and magistrates, but with the inclusion of independent members who were appointed by the chairman of the police authority. Not an ideal system perhaps, but certainly less politically slanted than the previous arrangements. Generally speaking, it seems that the police authorities had meaningful relationships with their chief constables and, to a large extent, the system worked well. The police authorities formed a collective (The Association of Police Authorities: APA) in order to harmonise policy and procedures; again this group generally worked well with the police. Progress on a range of topics became apparent, including community consultation, which was principally the responsibility of the police authorities. It then became a matter for the police authorities to hold the police themselves to account to ensure that they were involved and carried out the priorities identified by these consultative processes.

As already mentioned, 2012 saw the demise of the police authorities, to be replaced by elected police and crime commissioners (PCC's) with a more prescriptive system of public consultation; it was suggested that improved police accountability would follow these new appointments. Essentially, the PCC will be responsible for holding the police chief to account, setting the policing plan and budgets, engaging with the public, and engaging, or dismissing, the chief constable. The PCC will have a responsibility to publish results against the policing plan and this will be monitored through 'Police and Crime Panels' made up of a local government councillor and two independent, 'co-opted' persons. This system is still comparatively immature and how it will further develop and operate in practice remains to be seen, but it is difficult to appreciate what advantages will accrue that were not present through the system of police authorities. As with any system of external accountability, it's effectiveness will to some extent be a reflection of the structure, which in turn will constrain or facilitate desired outcomes. In the case of the PCC arrangements, it is likely that the success of individual police force accountability, including community consultation, will be significantly affected by the quality of the personal relationship between the chief constable and the PCC. That said, it is clear that the PCC's, especially those 'non-independents', will exercise a greater degree of political influence (control?) over the police than was the case with police authorities.

A great deal has been written about the so-called operational independence of chief constables and the commissioners in London, much of which seems fanciful. Quite clearly, police chiefs are accountable to politicians whether they like to admit it or not. The appointment of senior police officers necessitates the approval of a Home Office process as a significant feature of their selection. The office of the Inspectorate of Constabulary (HMIC) (now Her Majesty's Inspectorate of Constabulary, Fire, and Rescue Services,

HMICFRS) is a department of the Home Office that reports through the minister responsible for policing to the Home Secretary. It will be apparent, therefore, that if a particular police force was to be so aberrant with its policies and practices that the HMIPFR reported negatively, then it would only be a matter of time before the chief constable in question was held to account by the relevant minister. It is inconceivable that, in such circumstances, a police chief could lastingly oppose the spirit of government policy, procedure, and direction. In the final stages of such a divergence of views, the PCC could require the chief to resign. Conversely, if the chief enjoyed the support of the PCC, then the Home Office could withhold the taxpayers portion of the police budget until such time as its wishes were followed. This has never happened in recent times, but the powers undoubtedly exist to ensure that police chiefs can be held to account by the Home Office and thus central government politicians.

There has been much recent debate in both printed and broadcast media about the increasing involvement of politicians in policing, but it is really quite absurd for some police chiefs to claim they either have, or should have, autonomy and independence from political influence. Policing is a multi-million pound public service and obviously there is political influence over how such large sums are disbursed. To claim to the contrary is to unnecessarily create a constitutional argument with politicians that cannot be won. That said, police chiefs are necessarily the final arbiters of what gets investigated and what doesn't and typically politicians avoid becoming involved in such decisions. Recently, however, some high profile individuals have sought more influence here.

Traditionally, and by virtue of the Police Regulations that

are underpinned by primary legislation, police officers have been forbidden from taking an active part in politics. What exactly is meant by 'active' is not certain. Whether this amounts to simply being a member of a political party, or whether 'active' actually implies some physical or intellectual effort on behalf of a political party is equally unclear. What is certain, however, is that there was a specific intention to create a division between the work of police and those involved in politics. That is not to say that politicians should not be able to hold police to account for their decisions, but it is to prevent police officers selecting elements of their work that would play to the advantage of a particular political group or party that they favoured. For instance, facilitating or discouraging particular public protests, investigating particular types of crime in preference to others, allowing traffic congestion or the movement of goods to disadvantage a particular section of commercial activity. In all such matters, and many others besides, police are rightly expected, by most, to be impartial and not to be swayed by a particular political agenda. However, this expected political impartiality does not amount to a license for the police to do exactly as they want and to operate beyond political control. Therefore, for police chiefs and other senior officers to publicly make comments inferring their 'independence', or 'autonomy' is frankly ridiculous.

A problem with political accountability does emerge, however, if those providing the oversight of police forces (PCC's at present) exert their influence over the chief, or other police officers, to be selective as to what is done, or not done, that would favour a particular political agenda to the disadvantage of another. Here emerges the classic police dilemma in that it is impossible to please all the people all the time, but when operational discrimination starts to become consistently advantageous to some and disadvantageous to others, then political influence is probably having too great an affect.

There is no doubting that the introduction of PCC's to replace police authorities will bring a much closer political influence over policing. The majority of the new PCC appointments are individuals who openly represent a political party and, indeed, campaigned with the support of their parties. A number of independent candidates were elected in 2012 and the first round of re-elections has now taken place, both with a very small electoral turnout, and it might be reasonably assumed that where 'independents' were appointed, the electorate had difficulty in supporting a political appointee. That said, in those police districts where there are now elected and openly political PCC's elected by a similarly small electoral turnout, it is difficult to understand how these individuals' particular political views will not influence their judgment, despite frequent assertions and an oath to the contrary. These difficulties are likely to be most apparent in relation to budget disbursements. For instance, if a majority of politically active voters, who support the party of the PCC, reside in specific areas, it would be a challenge for a PCC to resist favouring a proportionally greater amount of a budget being expended from where supportive votes would be forthcoming. Simply, better levels of service in exchange for votes. Examples of such practices are widespread outside the UK. In many county sheriffs' departments in the USA, where the police chief is either an elected or a politically appointed person, police budgets are routinely focused on the areas, or priorities, that will attract the required voting preference. The logical and, to some extent, understandable extension of these practices, which may be observed in the USA, are the policing preferences given to the largest local taxpayers. Here again, a higher level of service is provided to those who contribute most, rather than to those who potentially have greater need of policing services, but who are without the financial or political influence to be a priority. Nothing here is intended to imply that the UK party political PCC's are lacking integrity, but it seems unlikely, given the competitive nature of party politics, that practices which are politically advantageous to them will not be followed in due course; time will tell.

It seems a further and potentially significant problem has been incorporated into the current arrangements for PCC's and this relates to the concept of personal accountability. It was previously mentioned that under the former arrangements, chief constables were accountable through the so-called tri-partite arrangement, one element of which was the personal accountability of the post holder. Now, though, effectively the person 'in charge' of a police force will be the PCC, as it will be this person who controls the budget and who appoints the chief. It appears that this appointee has little or no personal accountability. The only accountable responsibility upon a PCC being every five years through the ballot box. This contrasts sharply with the former routine, monthly police authority meetings and the continuous personal accountability of the chief constable. How it is proposed to hold PCC's to account in between the five year election intervals is unclear. Who, then, has the authority to dismiss a PCC who has been elected and under what circumstances? Ultimately, the Home Secretary will be the decision maker in this regard, which again brings political influence even closer to the operation and discharge of policing. In terms of personal accountability, it is apparent that the latest arrangements offer nothing in terms of improved personal accountability of those leading policing. In fact, quite the reverse.

This concept of personal accountability is important for a number of reasons. Personal accountability amounts to the difference between working at a job where the post holder is not obliged to explain the reasons for actions to those in receipt of the service, i.e. parcel delivery, private security guarding, hospitality services, and seemingly some aspects of health care. This is in contrast to those professions where there is either a legal or moral undertaking for the post holder to explain their actions and decisions, such as some of the regulated sectors; medicine, policing, legal services, etc. The attribute of personal accountability is one means of distinguishing between an occupation and a profession. However, it is tempting to comment that it seems some senior staff in sections of the financial services professions, although regulated, do not seem to be personally accountable for their decisions. In personal and practical terms, this obligation to be accountable is the difference between being committed to a satisfactory outcome and merely following a procedure or process. This is not to say that all individuals who are not personally accountable for their working actions do not provide a good service. It will be clear, however, that if an individual is habituated with the requirement of a need to be accountable on a routine basis, that responsibility becomes an internalised feature of working life. This must be very different from the obligation felt by, say, a PCC, who is not routinely and regularly accountable, such as a member of parliament, and who will only be measured in this regard at five year election intervals. This is a very different standard of policing accountability and one that surely is less convincing to the public than the previous system of police authorities. It is tempting to speculate that the real motive behind this change to PCC's was not of improving accountability of police chiefs, but one of increasing control by removing diverse and politically uncontrollable local police authorities.

At the heart of policing activity is, of course, the function of law enforcement. Here, police 'forces' and police officers are empowered to be the government's lawful civilian provider of force in pursuit of upholding the law. Of course, criminal and procedural legislation is full of checks and balances in this regard and concepts of 'reasonableness', 'proportionality', 'self-defence', 'protection of life', and similar are moderating factors that police must understand. However, no matter how well these concepts are understood, it is individual police officers themselves, who are legally accountable for decisions made in respect of the application of force as well as many other decisions that will be subsequently publicly tested in open court. The media regularly carry stories of police actions that are apparently open to question, often arising from highly conflictual situations in which police officers have to make rapid judgments about, amongst other things, the amount of force to be used in order to subdue a person or situation. Often months later, such decisions will be minutely dissected in calm, open court and every aspect of the context and circumstances will be reviewed. Fortunately, the vast majority of police decisions involving such judgments are not found to be wrong or misguided in any way. Sadly, the comparatively few actions and incidents that are either poorly judged, malicious, or erroneous result in both the individual officers and often the police leaders being held to further account by the police disciplinary process. The major point here, of course, is that the police are legally accountable for their actions as a distinct feature of their routine work. All police officers are well aware of this legal accountability and fortunately it is only relatively few occasions where this accountability is dishonoured, or that officers attempt to conceal the truth. When such circumstances are revealed, is hardly surprising that the sanctions and penalties imposed are typically and rightly severe. To breach the trust that the majority of the public invest in policing is not only a disservice to individuals involved in a particular situation, but arguably as importantly, a breach of the trust that police officers invest in their colleagues. It is the feature of legal accountability that provides the safeguards here.

It is fortunate that the concept of police legal accountability is taken so seriously, as the growing government tendency to centralise certain law enforcement activities effectively deprives local communities from having access to local accountability procedures. For instance, the activities of the Metropolitan Police in respect of national counter terrorism matters, the operations conducted by the National Crime Agency, as well as other centralised specialist units, such as the Serious Fraud Office (SFO) and the Competition and Markets Authority (CMA), are all accountable by law. It must also be noted, however, that each of these organisations and others that are similar in function, and have organisational accountability procedures in place, but the point is that these are difficult for the general public to access. This difficulty is compounded by distance from the capital and the bureaucracy that surrounds their operations, as well as, of course, the frequent necessity of secrecy. Such factors can give the impression that here are central law enforcement agencies who are not publicly accountable.

A public debate about 'local' police accountability rose in profile during government attempts to amalgamate provincial police forces in 2005/6. The principal issue that exercised the minds of those opposing amalgamations was that local police command would be removed from the identifiable areas in which they lived and with which they identified, such as existing county boundaries. The argument went that police headquarters would become remotely located, thus being less accessible, less responsive to particular local needs, and correspondingly less accountable to local people. These arguments proved to be persuasive, even in the face of the suggested economies that might be achieved, and the government abandoned the proposed changes. Much the same lines of argument have more recently been advanced to oppose the planned closure of many police stations, on the grounds of public spending economies. It remains to be seen whether or not the drivers for reducing public spending will succeed in overcoming the clear public preference for local police service delivery and local accountability.

It is to some extent a paradoxical situation that recent governments have created in respect of local police accountability. On the one hand, there is a clear movement towards more central government and thus political control over policing, but on the other, a very positive move towards and in support of 'Neighbourhood Policing' that sadly has now declined as a consequence of resource constraints (NP, Chapter Three).

NP took both the logic and the public preference for local police service delivery and local accountability to a practical solution. In summary, the NP design proposed a police team structure that would be responsible for a defined area, with local accountability provided through a system of police and public consultative groups. The organisational structural changes were to be supported by a computerised information system that would enable police to quickly identify when and where their services were most needed and where they should focus preventive measures. Despite a somewhat controversial early period of trials, NP was eventually pushed through into mainstream police thinking during the early 2000's and is now the preferred method of patrol and service delivery in cities and towns, as well as more rural areas. The difficulty remains, though, that despite creating a policing system that has local accountability at its core, communities' policing priorities are persistently over-ridden by those with a wider political agenda and the situation seems to be worsening in this regard. It seems to many that local policing, with local accountability, is the most desirable state of affairs, but the reality doesn't seem to follow the political rhetoric. Much of the evaluation material produced from the trials of NP and later research identified that the key to successful NP teams was maintaining adequate numbers of officers, who were available at identified key times, in order to avoid a return to simple response policing. This being the unplanned response to calls from the public, more or less according to reported seriousness, and in the timing and sequence of the report arrivals. Police attendance will, to some extent, depend on the availability of uncommitted police resources, rather than the reported priority of a call for assistance. Clearly, police controllers and call handlers will endeavour to re-prioritise calls for assistance when urgent emergencies occur, but it is frequently difficult to re-direct police officers once they have become engaged in the detail of another matter, albeit less urgent or demanding. For instance, it is very often not sensible to leave an ongoing neighbour dispute that has the potential to develop violently in order to deal with another matter, such as a more serious crime in progress. Of course, where life is thought to be in danger, then anything can be dropped and efforts re-directed to an emergency, but this will be dependent on the amount of information available to the police controller and dispatcher

Current government reductions in police numbers will inevitably encourage a situation in which police will only respond to specific types of calls from the public. Indeed, at the time of writing, several of the largest police forces have announced crime assessment policies, which in effect means that crimes considered to be minor and where there is little prospect of obtaining any evidence, they will not be investigated. Retail thefts, minor damage, and minor fraud are all likely to depart from police attention. Such policies are considered in more detail in Chapter Six, but one of the consequences will be that responding officers will have only passing identity and association with the individuals and the communities with whom they react and the outcome will be very little local accountability. So, the public lose out on both counts; little local service delivery and little accountability.

Quite reasonably and rightly, when this gloomy prediction comes to pass, the media will make much of the poor state of policing affairs. Thus the role of the media might be regarded as a further element in the issue of police accountability. From the days not so long ago, when the local court reporter was a major contributor to small local newspapers, to the high speed electronic news industry of today, policing news has always been in demand. It is hardly surprising, therefore, that over recent decades, police officers and journalists have forged close relationships that have benefited each other. Indeed, in many matters, police officers and journalists share similar curiosity and possess a similar desire for righteous outcomes. Journalistic investigations are not, of course, subject to the same rules of evidence that guide police investigations. This doesn't mean that journalists can do whatever they want, but it does allow a greater freedom that arises because, generally, their information will not be used as evidence. For those police officers who are privileged to have a close relationship with a particular journalist, this situation can provide police with valuable intelligence, given the absolute necessity to preserve sources on both sides

For the police side, journalists will regularly run stories designed to stimulate interest in a particular matter in order to elicit witnesses and further information. For the journalist, an interesting story is provided which will often contain the essential 'human interest' component. So, whilst this relationship might be described as at least, partially symbiotic, there are nevertheless many strains and stresses to be overcome for each to experience satisfaction from the relationship. Principal amongst the irritations experienced by police at the hands of the media is their role to hold the police to account. It is a perfectly reasonable and a valuable function of a free media to expect police to account for their actions and decisions and to add comment on these. Indeed, it is what the general public have come to expect. This can, however, produce defensiveness in the minds of some police officers that can grow to destructively cynical attitudes as to motives of the media industry as a whole and to individual journalists. Despite the challenges in sustaining good police/media relations, however, it remains vital that the media continues to have the confidence to hold police to account. It is only in this way that the police might come to better understand changing attitudes in communities and society as a whole. It is only too easy for the police to consider that they 'know best' when it comes to dealing with the ills of society and it is a most useful function of the media to remind police that this is not necessarily so. There has been much debate and enquiry surrounding topics associated with the police/media relationship during the recent past. Suffice to say here that police accountability through the media has been, and should continue to be a vital feature of the means by which police are held to account.

It does seem as though the topic of police accountability will not lose profile over the coming years. The last government was rightly committed to improving police performance and accountability, but the means they chose to achieve this did seem to lack any real chance of doing so. The priorities are clear: the public expect to know who is responsible for policing activities and service delivery, they prefer the structure of police forces to be identifiable with communities, they expect policing to be of high quality and accountable. Given that all these aspirations are achievable, it is not difficult to design appropriate policies, structures, and systems to deliver these operational outcomes within economic constraints. The means of achieving these changes are explored in chapters five and six.

More controversial, however, is the method by which whole police forces are governed. Some description was given in Chapter Three of recent structures that have been implemented for this purpose. What will now be clear, however, is that governance and accountability are topics that cannot be separated; the latter depending in large part on the former. It has been shown that addressing a community's priorities is a major component of UK policing and is a very good reason for government not having direct operational control of the function. However, it is also apparent that accountability issues and the identification of priorities has become increasingly obscure to the public. It was suggested that the passing of formalised 'Police Community Consultative Groups' contributed to this situation without any effective replacement. Now it is even more apparent that many societal groupings feel marginalised from policing because sufficient attention or importance is not given to their particular needs. Female victimisation, issues arising from the lesbian, bi-sexual, gay and transgender groups (LGBT), black, Asian, and visible mixed race individuals and communities are all examples of people that, to a greater or lesser extent, might have reason to doubt the quality of service they receive from the police. A minor defence of the police position is that it is not always possible to know or to predict exactly what is required. Conversely, some signals are clear and strong but are consistently ignored or marginalised by police.

The following proposal therefore attempts to provide a model to re-establish the direct influence of all communities and society as a whole, offer transparency to police activity and priority setting, whilst providing a mechanism that is distant from political control, but exercising effective governance.

It has been suggested that elected Police and Crime Commissioners (PCCs) are a part of the described problem situation. However, it is also clear that, as a political initiative, they should form a part of the solution. So, it is proposed that their role should be altered to become the chair of a committee/authority for each (regional?) police force. The various support facilities and oversights with whom PCCs currently operate should fall aside and be replaced with a full-time executive support group. Under the direction of the PCC, the support group would seek out and invite representatives of specific interest groups to attend regular police oversight meetings, say every month, together with a few representatives of local authorities and other statutory service providers, such as health care, social services, CPS, courts, etc. depending on local need and to balance special needs with the 'common good'.

Membership would be a matter for local decision depending on local circumstances. For instance, a more rural policing area may need the advice of a farming or veterinary specialist, whereas a more urban area may value a noise abatement member or drug rehabilitation specialist. The emphasis should be on providing an accountability forum for current policing priorities. Membership might change over time, depending on local circumstances, and this would be a matter for the PCC to decide who should also have the opportunity of seeking the attendance of police officers who can contribute relevant knowledge and experience, not only the chief constable with his/her senior team.

Simply, this proposal is a synergy of the defunct consultative groups with the previous model for police authorities, without the constrained or prescribed membership of both.

The equally controversial role of the PCC is the power to select and dismiss a chief constable. It is inevitable that personal and perhaps political opinions will have a dysfunctional influence on this particular responsibility. It is almost certain that, in selecting a chief constable, a PCC will take account of the personal political views of an aspirant chief, whether such views are elicited by questioning or through previous public expressions by the officer. However such an opinion is formed, it is clear that a PCC will have a political platform and will seek a chief who follows that particular political line. Whether such congruity is sufficient to sustain a productive relationship is unclear, but it seems that either a chief will have a strong and productive relationship with their PCC, or the opposite will develop whereby the actions and decisions of each will be criticised by the other. In the event of a harmonious relationship, any inappropriate decisions and actions could possibly be ignored or 'smoothed over', whereas in a more conflictual relationship, such matters may form the basis of a disproportionate sanction at worst, or at best a continuing decline in mutual respect.

In either case, the outcome is less than satisfactory. It is suggested that this particular function is removed from PCC's and replaced by a national assessment and qualification process which is objectively based on previous performance, experience, and ability. HM Inspectorate of Constabulary (HMICFRS) could have a key role here on behalf of the Home Office, which in turn would provide an imperative to both chief constables and PCC's to make their relationship open, productive, and harmonious.

5.

Police Operations

What the cops actually do

Chapter One reviewed the nature of the work of the police and touched on some of the tasks that constitute the daily challenges. As any regular television viewer will know, police work is hugely varied and often emotionally demanding, which is probably why there have been so many popular television series devoted to policing and investigations of all types. So, here and in the following chapter, the reality of this work will be reviewed and a model of how future police functions might be arranged will be proposed. The demands on police from public events, patrol, the initial stages of crime investigations, and crime prevention are discussed.

When the NP project was originally devised during 1981 (Chapter Three), a good deal of attention was given to the benefits of so called 'community policing' and the potential impact that such a strategy might have on the incidence of crime and anti-social behaviour. Community policing became fashionable in many police areas in response to public criticism of a system known as 'unit beat policing' (UBP). This system essentially provided small cars (panda cars) in which a large proportion of uniform officers with personal radios could patrol and respond to calls for assistance. The initiative was greatly assisted by the implementation of locally operated personal radio systems, which effectively meant that patrolling police could be directed to wherever there was a problem, reflecting the public value of the police response function. The criticism centred on the separation that quickly developed between the police and the public. Even communities in urban areas had been used to seeing and speaking with their local officers in high streets and other populated places, so when UBP drew them away from this more personal style of foot or bicycle patrol, understandably there was much concern.

Community policing therefore offered a means by which both methods of patrol might be used. Officers could promptly respond to calls for assistance, but also park their highly visible cars in populated places and patrol the same locality regularly on foot and thus becoming known to the community; the reality was, of course, that the police officers largely remained in their cars! More importantly, though, the community policing thinking was that routine and regular police association with a particular community would give the police a better opportunity to gain information about who was causing trouble and committing crimes, thus providing the police with the necessary intelligence information to intervene earlier than might otherwise have been possible. This information was to be recorded and collated at local police stations so that it would be available to influence community involvement, local patrols, and interventions. So, the benefit of crime prevention was recognised as a means of reducing the demands on police, which was basically the reason for the introduction of UBP.

The designers of NP, who endeavoured to quantify the preventive benefits of police patrol, did not ignore these issues. In doing so, a model was developed that simply showed that if police ignored proactive, preventive measures as a part of the patrol function, then demands on their services would increase. There is research to show that the mere presence of a uniformed police patrol will not prevent crime in itself, but probably displace it to another location. However, if the patrolling officer engages with potential victims and is alert to the opportunities for crime and disorder, then the community will be more responsive in assisting. Stimulating the community in such ways to involve themselves in improving their quality of life was at the heart of the 'community policing' philosophy, and this was developed by the NP designers into a more prescriptive model for police patrols whereby police were trained to use intelligence and other data to achieve results. It was proposed that the outcome of the NP initiative, if fully implemented, would be a reduction, or at least a steadying, in the response demands on police, which hitherto had been relentlessly spiralling upwards. In the areas where the NP system was trialled, this was certainly the case and the effect of the so called 'reactive spiral' was shown to have been moderated, in as much that the rate of increase of response demands was reduced. The NP scheme subsequently became known as 'sector policing' in London and was adopted in many parts of the country, as it was seen to offer an improved deployment system with some prospect of containing ever increasing demands, without losing contact with the public. Gratefully, the title 'Neighbourhood Policing' has been re-adopted and is now a very commonly used term within the policing vocabulary

What actually followed in order to slow this spiralling demand increase was, however, not nearly as positive in relation to coping with increasing crime and anti-social behaviour. A so-called 'crime screening system' imported from the USA was adopted by many police forces. Simply, statistical weights were ascribed to various features of a reported crime and a final, weighted score determined whether the incident would receive a police response, or be investigated at all. For example, if a car was stolen from outside a house, the victim would be asked if there were any witnesses and when the car was stolen, whether it was locked, and so on. If the response was that these details were unknown, or were vague, then it would be considered that there was no prospect of solving the matter promptly, so there would be nothing to be gained by dispatching an officer to examine a space on the road where the car had been parked. This, of course, ignores the possibility that if an officer visited then scene, then enquiries might be made of neighbours, the roadside might be searched for any traces of the thief, dropped articles, etc. and it might be possible to determine whether the thief was a passer-by, or from a nearby location. By not attending the scene, the police almost totally deprive themselves of any opportunity of solving the crime. Merely waiting until the stolen car is abandoned is hardly the way to give the victim any confidence that the matter is being dealt with professionally. This type of case screening system was adopted and used in respect of many incidents and events reported to the police, doubtless leaving a large number of disgruntled victims. The effect of such indifferent police response can be shown to have a very limiting influence on the victims' propensity to assist police in the future. Members of the public who put themselves forward as witnesses to events, or who become actively involved in crime prevention schemes, such as neighbourhood watch, property marking events, etc. do so because they feel a civic duty to do so and that they are supported by the police. On the contrary, communities ignored by police do not feel obliged to become involved in any way and leave all such matters to the police alone, who of course are less than effective without the active involvement of the public.

There is an irony that emerged from the experiences of case screening systems in that, a decade or so later, another strategic initiative imported from the USA was known as 'zero tolerance'. The approach here was for police to deal strictly with all crimes and regulation breaches, so even the most minor offence, or attempted offence, would be prosecuted through the justice system. The thinking was that if the police and community exhibited a complete intolerance towards crime and misbehaviour, then potential offenders would be deterred from committing these and other anti-social acts. As might have been foreseen, there are several serious flaws with this approach so far as UK society and, by extension, UK policing are concerned. A large number of generally law abiding people become caught up in a system that shows no discretion or tolerance of minor infringements, leading to an unsympathetic view of police and policing with a potentially negative opinion of the law makers. Police are perceived as dealing with minor issues in preference to more complex, demanding, and serious matters; this stimulates a general intolerance for police activity. Furthermore, police resources that were already stretched have to accommodate a much greater throughput of case files, leading to an overburdening of the whole police organisation. Conceptually, of course, there is no logical limit to zero tolerance and the consequence of pursuing such a strategy for any length of time would be to necessitate a huge increase in police capacity. This, of course, was satisfied in the USA; where zero tolerance initiatives were implemented, the strategy was accompanied by significant increases in front line police numbers. With hindsight, it does seem somewhat perverse that in order to limit response demands on the police, one tactic was to simply screen out demand and the other to actively increase it. Needless to say, both systems were abject failures; the public being the sufferers in both instances.

It is interesting to note that, several decades later, some police forces, including London's Metropolitan Police, have re-introduced a crime screening model (under a different name) to exclude minor, low value, low impact reports from investigative attention. Apparently, this will allow officers to spend more time on more serious matters and, given the strain on resources, the policy is claimed to be an inevitability. This does, of course, ignore most of the lessons from the previous adventures into such schemes as described above.

These experiments lead back to the inescapable concept of policing by consent and police involving communities in both crime prevention and detection. As noted previously, there is a clear expectation from the public that police will assist and be compassionate when they become victims and be robust in tackling their priorities against criminals. On the part of the police, it is assumed that the public will be supportive of police operations and be willing witnesses in return.

In order to meet these demands and expectations, it is important that police resources are optimally deployed, but regrettably this is seldom the case. Typically, in cities, towns, and more urban areas, uniformed police staff are divided into four numerically equivalent work groups, variously called sections, reliefs, groups, or similar. The eight hour working day is divided into three shifts, early seven a.m. to three p.m., late three p.m. to eleven p.m., and night eleven p.m. to seven a.m., or closely similar times. A duty rota allocates the work groups to the three daily shifts, the fourth having a rest day, with the pattern generally rotating through a four week period. Each work group therefore experiences the same number of shifts of different times and has the same number of rest days. Adjustments can made to cater for particular local needs, but generally speaking, something similar to this rotating pattern, or duty rota, is the means by which police performing response and patrol duties are deployed. The obvious advantages are that the system is quite straightforward to administer, police officers are able to work out well in advance when they will have a day off, or be working a particular shift. A strong team spirit develops between officers working together in their particular group, which is beneficial in so far as job satisfaction and mutual support is concerned. That, however, is where the advantages end; in some respects, the strong team culture has the potential of fostering the development of mis-placed loyalties, such as concealing mistakes or wrong doing by team colleagues.

In terms of operational effectiveness, such a rigid system is inappropriate in most circumstances. Demands on police vary according to the day of the week, the time of the day, and the location. So, for instance, a system in a town that deploys the same number of officers at six a.m. on a weekday morning, as at midnight on a Saturday night, is likely to have idle staff at one time whilst leaving others very stretched when demands are high. Very often, local arrangements are made to partially correct this problem, but the rules for designing these rota systems are enshrined in the statutory Police Regulations. These regulations, at minimum, require the acceptance of the Home Secretary to amend and the agreement of Parliament to change if the primary legislation is to be altered. This in turn necessitates a consultation process with the police staff associations, who have shown themselves very resistant to modernising these duty rota or rest day systems, as they are known. This is hardly surprising, as it is the clear mandate of the police staff associations, as with any other staff association, to protect and enhance the working conditions of its members. It is clear, however, that in order to achieve the most productive deployment of police, duty periods, including start and finish times, must be more flexible, be closer aligned to local demands, and with the opportunity to make changes without necessitating severe financial compensation.

In more rural areas, the past has seen police officers deployed from police owned houses and working alongside the community in which they live, often having considerable discretion over their times of duty. However, this practice has largely fallen away due, if for no other reason, to the cost of providing and maintaining such accommodation. As with the urban deployment system, it was also undeniably the case that many officers working these detached rural areas had large amounts of unproductive, if not idle, time. Clearly, they needed to be more closely associated with their urban colleagues and accept a greater share of the workload.

However, the closure of these detached rural sections, the closure of many small police offices in villages, and more recently the closure of police stations in towns and cities has exacerbated the problems of the duty rota system. For instance, when information arrives requiring a police response, there is likely to be some travelling time involved and this in itself will occupy a police officer in unproductive activity for longer than might otherwise have been the case. It may indeed create a reluctance to attend certain incidents due to the return travel time and the need to restrict overtime costs, or to leave work punctually for a private commitment.

Police are deployed to incidents largely as a result of information or requests by telephone. Depending on the nature of the incident, a police control room[4] operator will make a decision as to the most appropriate police response. A low key incident, involving, say, a minor dispute might attract a single police officer, whereas a major disturbance involving large numbers of alcohol-influenced revellers may well attract a van full of police, if available. Similarly, specialist police units will be sent to particular types of incident, such as those where reportedly firearms or other weapons are seen or thought to be involved. However, all initial deployments are dependent on the accuracy of the incoming information and the ability of control room staff to properly appreciate what is happening, or has happened. This, of course, is not always possible as very often those who contact police for assistance are traumatised in some way, excited, nervous, anxious, or simply unclear about what is happening. For instance, what sounds like gunshots in a town, persistent screaming, or someone sprinting away from an apparently collapsed person might all have perfectly reasonable, lawful explanations. All such incidents, however, potentially necessitate a police response, but very often the job of the police initially deployed will be to find out exactly what has occurred and then to organise appropriate back up, or supplementary resources, to efficiently cope with whatever has happened. This is not always a straightforward task; assessing situations takes diligence and experience, so it becomes most important for the control room dispatcher to ensure, as far as

---

[4] *(Information room/operations room /control room/call centre, are used interchangeably)*

possible, that the most appropriate resource is deployed. The police success in dealing with more serious incidents is frequently determined by the actions of the officer, or officers, making the initial response. It is important to recognise this vital aspect of response operations, as much as the investigative work that follows will be dependent on initial efforts and assumptions; more will be added to this topic in the following chapter.

As well as the routine patrol function and the response demands on police that occur throughout the day and night, the police are the principal resource for providing safety and organisation of public events. Such occasions are quite diverse in character and include pre-planned demonstrations, fetes, carnivals, shows, open air concerts, processions, and similar, as well as many sporting events, both those contained in stadia and those played in public places. Generally, events that take place in private grounds and stadia are managed and organised by the relevant sporting organisations and owners of the grounds, with stewarding and management being provided by the organisers' staff, or by private security companies. However, the public places aspect of these events becomes the responsibility of the police. So, crowd movement to and from a venue is planned, controlled, and marshalled by the police. This, of course, can place an enormous burden on police resources and significantly reduce the numbers of officers and PCSO's available for work at other times. The planning processes for such events are also time consuming and, in some cases, extremely lengthy and with demanding activity, especially in respect of those protest demonstrations where the organisers are frequently not minded to co-operate with police planning. Adequate preparation is vital however and clear plans need to be understood by all police assets. Briefings, training, and clear communication are of course essential as failure in this regard will certainly result in chaos and, at worst, in casualties. Indeed, a highly respected senior officer once remarked that, "...public [dis]order policing is the hardest thing police do."

Closely associated with public events policing, in terms of degrees of difficulty and uncertainty, is the policing of crowded places. Naturally, it follows that many of the policies, best practices, and tactics deployed for public events similarly apply to the concept of other crowded places, such as transport hubs; typically large railway stations, airports, motorway service areas, and similar. The concept also applies to retail and shopping centres, Christmas fairs and markets, in fact anywhere large numbers of people gather together. The problems of policing such areas will be obvious; many people in a restricted area provide an ideal target for terrorists and thieves and a difficult environment in which effective preventive or reassurance policing can take place. The application of technology, especially closed circuit television and video surveillance, provides what seems to be a continuously improving methodology for crowd monitoring. Such methods are, of course, useless unless there are police officers deployed and able to respond to the video monitoring where, say, a pick-pocketing gang is identified, or more worryingly, suspects are identified in activities that appear to be about preparation for an attack.

A consequence of insufficient officers available to deal with the full range of policing tasks is encapsulated in the recurring theme of this book; the regrettable shift away from Neighbourhood Policing (NP). This trend inevitably results in a slide back to mainly reactive methods, where officers spend the majority of time responding to calls for assistance, leaving little opportunity for pro-active preventive tactics, with the attendant reduction in the confidence of the public that the police can actually deal with criminality. There cannot be a more striking example of this shift than the recent (2021) highly damaging loss of confidence in policing by many women following a series of high profile, serious personal attacks that the police have not handled effectively. NP would have likely provided several advantages that would have avoided both this reduction in confidence and a more effective response. Firstly, an opportunity to better understand current and increasing problems through the availability of a less formal channel for bringing issues to the notice of police. Secondly, it would enable the police to deploy preventive and reassurance tactics in a specific locality, as well as providing more detailed information in support of a more focused reactive response. Each of these tactics would enhance confidence in policing as opposed to the opposite. It would not be an exaggeration to say that this loss of confidence that has developed has reached crises proportions and an effective strategy is needed immediately to rectify the problem and reverse this trend.

Clearly, as with other policing tasks, adequately trained and experienced officers are necessary to tackle the issue effectively, but much should be done now to restore female public confidence and halt this negative trend. A strategy for achieving this might be presented in two parts. Firstly, a preventive effort to re-establish a positive feeling of public safety for women and, secondly, a re-appraisal of how police deal with crimes reported by females who are victims.

Highly visible preventive patrolling at busy and crowded times and places should be improved. Closing times of pubs, clubs, other places of entertainment, large shopping centres, and public transport hubs are obvious examples of locations for short or static foot patrols supported by reactive back-up to swiftly deal with all sorts of anti-social behaviour, but especially giving close attention to female vulnerability. For instance, being visible and approachable to receive complaints of crimes or other anti-social behaviour. In a similar vein, visible reassurance patrolling at crowded places with police engagement with potential female targets and giving advice respecting appropriate safety measures. Advice given in this way is more effective than publicity campaigns. For instance, carrying bags safely, not displaying victim behaviours, encouraging visible mobile phone use, avoiding direct eye contact, etc. More complicated preventive tactics might be discussed with police at women's clubs, societies, and sports clubs, such as double back techniques to identify stalkers, use of well-lit and busy thoroughfares, and heightened awareness of victim behaviours. Police might also join with the responsible employers who routinely provide personal safety and crime prevention courses for their staff.

Turning to reactive tactics, reports to police of stalking, unwanted attention, indecent exposure, suspicious behaviour, and suchlike must be recorded and where necessary investigated. Where an investigation is not called for, but the complaint could be an indicator or predictor of future unwanted actions, patrols should be briefed with descriptions and locations and the report statistics carefully monitored by supervisors. Local intelligence records should be compiled and maintained on the basis of this information, with onward referrals made when wider patterns are discerned. Patrol deployments might be adjusted to correspond to identified likely problem locations where high visibility police presence would have a positive preventive effect. Where appropriate, covert methods might be adopted with a view to either gathering further intelligence or apprehending offenders.

Where a crime is committed and the victim is female, it is important that appropriately trained and experienced officers undertake the investigation. For instance, in the case of rape allegations, the investigating officer should be at least the rank of detective inspector, as such individuals will have received advanced investigation training, including sexual assault matters, forensic opportunities, and have the necessary seniority to deploy appropriate resources to the case. The CPS have specialist rape case lawyers and crown court judges need a 'rape ticket' to try such cases, so there is no reason for the police not to apply similar importance to rape allegations. Similarly, with other serious offences, such wounding or homicide, senior police leaders should ensure that appropriately experienced and qualified officers, especially if they are female, are in control of such investigations; indeed, regular and direct oversight of such matters by chief officers is highly beneficial, especially when there are limited lines of enquiry. For less serious allegations, the investigating officers should preferably be female with appropriate training, with victims receiving attention from victim support officers or volunteers for as long as necessary. Such attention will provide an opportunity, with the confidence of victims, to reveal any further, unreported offences, such as women who have experienced serial domestic violence

Much good work has been undertaken by the police in respect of such incidents and events, but repetitive incidents directed at vulnerable victims, such as women on their own, inevitably attract calls for more attention. Considerable experience has been acquired that enables police to provide the necessary coverage at locations considered to be vulnerable. Generally, the major events that characterise the country are policed safely and reassuringly by low key operations that facilitate events, rather than cause a hindrance. Suffice to say that crowds, wherever they gather and for whatever purpose, will always have the attention of those who wish the country and its population harm. However, there is nothing that should prevent the police from deploying similar tactics, as described above, to provide protection and reassurance for vulnerable groups.

Roads and traffic policing continues to be a vital function for police. As has been noted previously, many routine responses on motorways are now undertaken by Highways Agency patrols. However, serious and fatal injury collisions require the investigative skills of police officers and very often the police forensic evidence gathering capability with collision analysis methodologies. Similarly, many criminals travel on roads between their diverse activities and attract the attention of roads policing officers who will also give attention to driving regulation enforcement, such as speeding, alcohol/drug driving, etc. The use of expertly ridden police-marked motor cycles continue to be a valuable capability for the security of vulnerable persons and cargo in transit.

It might be appreciated that the functions of uniform police are vital to the confidence the public are entitled to have in their policing systems. Yet it is apparent that the officers delivering these services are constrained by archaic regulations, which in many ways restrict the way in which police might be deployed. It is clear that the only sensible way to correct these, and many other problems that arise from inflexible working regulations, is to completely overhaul the conditions of work for police officers and make them more in line with modern commercial working practices.

The payment of overtime is anachronistic for supposedly professional police. The insistence on a fixed duty rota pattern is unreasonable in the light of the clear public need for efficient response services. And to deploy officers in such a way as to separate them from contact with the public is to ignore the lessons of the past. All this, together with the need to demonstrate good value for the taxpayer, requires a different way of thinking about the police role. Police officers are quite rightly forbidden from striking and are financially compensated for this, but they also cannot be dismissed unless they have been through the quasi-judicial disciplinary process, and their post cannot be made redundant. In other words, it is a very secure occupation and it is imminently possible for a uniformed officer to contribute very little effort and remain employed. This situation surely cannot be tolerated in circumstances where the quality of service delivery is the priority.

6.

Crime Investigations

What detectives actually do.

A major operational function of police is to investigate alleged criminality and, where evidence can be found, to bring forward cases to the Crown Prosecution Service (CPS) for consideration of prosecution. As already explained, a limited amount of less serious investigative work is routinely carried out by uniformed officers, who also have other responsibilities, but the bulk of the investigations into more serious alleged criminal matters is undertaken by trained detectives who customarily spend their duty time in plain clothes. These officers are drawn from applicants from the uniform branch. Normally, there is a period of local assessment of suitability for investigative work, followed by a series of training courses to fully equip detectives to tackle the most intricate and complex investigations. Further training courses are available to prepare officers for more specialist crime investigations, such as child and sexual offences, rape, murder, economic crime/fraud, counter terrorism, and other matters that require either specialist knowledge or particular skills.

    A very clear and consistent trend that has been apparent for several decades is the tendency for detectives to leave mainstream, but varied, investigative work to specialise in very specific types of crime investigation. This trend has been primarily driven by the increasing complication and sophistication of some crimes and the pressure to respond more effectively to some types of criminality. For instance, counter terrorism activity, international organised crime, embracing money laundering and human trafficking, international fraud, so-called 'hate crimes', and of course the priority to protect children and young people from the attentions of sexual predators. This trend might be further illustrated by the growing need for police to tackle crime facilitated through the internet. In response, many forces now have dedicated 'high-tech', 'e-crime', or cyber-crime units that have refined investigative skills to tackle some of the growing abuses of this medium and the associated applications. It will be apparent that it takes a good deal of time and training to assimilate the necessary skills and expertise to tackle many of these more specialised crimes that simply cannot be tackled effectively by general duty investigators. It follows that having expended considerable resources training officers to undertake such specialist investigations, there is little management logic to moving officers away from such roles. The argument is often advanced that specialists need to move around to gain wider experiences, but identifying officers with the correct aptitude, training them, and the time to gain experience outweighs the somewhat old fashioned notion of multiple competencies. Additionally, there is the important activity of network building, whereby officers develop a range of contacts in partner organisations which facilitate each other's activities. For instance, economic crime investigators will need to have contacts with the Serious Fraud Office and counter terrorism officers will need to be familiar with the role of the Security Service. Such contacts take time to establish and yet more time to develop the trust and knowledge to make the network productive. If officers are working energetically and capably, it makes no sense at all to keep moving them around, driven by a career development policy that favours generalists. However, despite the efficiency benefits of specialisation discussed in Chapter Two, the managerial logic of training and keeping specialist investigators allocated to their chosen specialisation has to be balanced against the tendency of some specialists to become over focused on their particular discipline to the detriment of other aspects of police work. This usually manifests as an intolerance of other aspects of police work and a lack of understanding of wider police functions and public expectations. In the worst manifestation of such over-specialisation, officers display an unjustified arrogance, frequently using pejorative and demeaning language towards colleagues who they perceive as having lesser roles than themselves.

Surprisingly, some might argue, detectives working in territorial police forces are paid the same as their uniform colleagues, with a few minor exceptions, and are subject to the same police regulations effectively regulating their working conditions and practices, in much the same way as other police officers.

Generally, detectives' times of duty will be governed locally, with officers being available at the busiest times, whilst others pursue their case enquiries during day and evening shifts. Investigations are customarily allocated on the basis of the anticipated workload involved and the skills or experience thought to be required in any particular case. This is not a process that lends itself to the specification of a clear policy, but rather the attention of a senior and experienced investigator, who will be aware of the likely challenges presented by any particular crime. On the basis of this scrutiny of allegations, detectives' supervisors are able to monitor progress and offer advice in any particular set of circumstances; good teamwork being essential at all times. Whilst there tends to be more flexibility in detectives' duty rotas to facilitate their work, these plans are frequently thrown into disarray when a serious crime, such as a murder, is revealed. In such circumstances, the investigation is progressed by officers drawn from routine detective duties under the leadership of a senior investigating officer, who would typically be a detective chief inspector or detective superintendent. Such arrangements are inevitable in order to adequately resource major investigations, but the withdrawal of detectives from routine investigations does cause an enormous amount of frustration at the local level, where work simply cannot be progressed within expected times. It is only in the much larger police forces where there are permanent teams of detectives dedicated to investigating specific and serious crimes, such as murder. It is now, however, commonly the practice to establish inter-force, service level agreements in order to deal with the more serious and specialised types of crimes. Similarly, regional serious crime teams and counter terrorist units are a common feature of the police preparedness to respond to such events.

One of the major problems in the lives of detectives, whether they are operating from a local police station or a detached specialist unit, is that there is no predictable limit to the demand for their services. Routine work can sometimes proceed at a manageable pace for weeks, or even months, but then a series of serious crimes, or incidents can disrupt carefully organised workloads by drawing officers away from their planned work. There is really no easy solution to this problem; it is simply not realistic to have trained detectives sitting around waiting for major crimes to be reported so they can promptly respond. It seems inevitable that, as more serious events occur, the more common and arguably less serious matters will be investigated in longer time scales, to the consequential frustration of others, especially victims. Similarly, there is often no predictable limit to the complexity of some investigations. It is not unusual for a crime that initially appears to be straightforward, to turn into a far reaching and major investigation. This often occurs where a series of similar crimes have been committed, sometimes in different parts of the country, when detectives then have to spend a good deal of unplanned time understanding and connecting linked events. This work carries the attendant difficulties of identifying and securing evidence in order to present a report of the sequence of events. Such investigations call for a meticulous attention to detail and are, by their very nature, time consuming, demanding, and require careful coordination. Likewise, much time can be expended on major international investigations that present no realistic prospect of securing a conviction in a UK court, due to the difficulties of securing and presenting evidence from non UK jurisdictions. A very great deal of time and effort can be expended on this type of enquiry in the mistaken belief that members of some major criminal organisation might be brought to justice. Recent high profile examples demonstrate that the reality of such efforts is far from the initial ambitions.

These two characteristics of unlimited demand and unforeseen complexity make for a great deal of disruption to the private lives of the investigators, who from time to time might spend more time away from their homes than they might have chosen. Compensation for such work beyond a forty-hour week is by way of overtime payments, up to the rank of chief inspector, with the corresponding impact on local and force level budgets if adequate provision has not been made for major enquiries. Quite why such a scheme of remuneration has persisted for so long is quite absurd. Police detectives, together with their colleagues in other branches of police work, are highly trained professionals and should be rewarded by means of a fixed salary. Those not wishing to commit to the vagaries of the work and lifestyle would perhaps be well advised to seek alternative employment; there will certainly be no shortage of keen recruits and aspirants to take their place.

As will be evident, there is a finite number of officers who have the necessary skills and experience to carry out efficient investigative work and, as previously discussed, the increasing trend that necessitates officers to 'super specialise' has a marked effect on the numbers of detectives available for routine work. Clearly. there is also the consequential, negative impact on front line uniform officer numbers, which is the pool from where all detectives are currently initially drawn. There have been a number of initiatives to tackle this problem of the abstraction of officers for specialist or major investigations, amongst which was the concept of the 'omni-competent' police officer. Simply, the idea was to improve the skills training of as many officers as possible so that crime investigations might be taken on by more officers, thus spreading the load. The difficulty, of course, being that if officers spend time undertaking anything but the most straightforward enquiries, their availability for patrol and response activity becomes limited. It is clear, therefore, that the reactive loop model presented by the NP project, which described in straightforward terms the inescapable conclusion that unless more effort and resources are put into crime prevention, demands on the police will always rise to exceed the capacity of available police resources.

Two further limitations are common to many investigations; that of investigative adherence to a particular theory without any apparent evidence and the associated preoccupation with theories of the criminals' motivation. Both these phenomena are equally futile and can consume a disproportionate level of resources for very little progress in return. In the first instance, the golden rule for an investigator is to be guided by the evidence, not by some vague theory that seems plausible and to persuasively fit the circumstances, but without any supporting or corroborating evidence. Regarding the question of the perpetrator's motivation, in many serious crimes it will be apparent that the motivation would be compelling for the perpetrator, but very difficult for the investigator to appreciate; here again, the most productive strategy is to follow the evidence, keep an open mind, and search for the truth, rather than consume disproportionate resources trying to divine a motivation which, in so many cases, will be outside the understanding of the investigation team. For instance, how would a naturally sane police officer understand the motive of a psychopathic killer or child molester?

As more and more time passes during the course of a criminal investigation, either due to a shortage of resources or some procedural difficulty, the more difficult it becomes to discover new evidence, or indeed to maintain the integrity of evidence already revealed. Witnesses become less convincing, victims become frustrated and angry at the speed of justice, and in the worst examples of dilatory investigations, the case becomes incapable of successful prosecution. It seems that delays have been tolerated at all stages in the criminal prosecution process and that this tolerance has created a culture that views such practice as normal and unavoidable. The police claim that adequate resources are being applied to a particular investigation in the context of the pressure to meet other demands. The CPS claim that it takes time for lawyers to scrutinise the police file, seek adjustments or further enquiries, and come to a decision. In more serious cases, the CPS then have to instruct counsel to present the case in the higher courts and this, it is argued, takes more time. The matter is then listed by the Court Service for preliminary hearing and eventually a date is set for a trial; it is possible for the whole process to drag on for months and sometimes years. Meanwhile, those involved move on with their work and lives, returning to the case in court some considerable time after the event.

Delays created by a variety of reasons almost inevitably bring costs, whether these are direct costs for, say, additional time incurred by both prosecution and defence lawyers, police opportunity costs arising from additional officer time devoted to the case, or indeed the costs to the courts arising from adjournments. There are also costs in non-monetary terms, which may be just as significant, such as victim and witness stress and of course the natural anxiety of the accused. The surprising thing is, however, that whilst all these additional costs affect practically everyone involved in the criminal trial process, it seems there is no motivation to resolve the difficulties. Cynically, it might be proposed that it is not in the financial interest of the barristers and instructing solicitors to speed things along, but this is hardly the whole picture. Delays affect most individuals and organisations connected with a criminal case, one way or another, and it would seem an obvious step to try to take a collective approach to reducing these negative effects, but yet they persist.

The currently (2018) controversial issue of the failure of police and prosecutors to fully disclose evidence to suspects, or their defence, has raised issues concerning this legal requirement, principal amongst which is the delay incurred in the criminal justice process. Simply, revelation and disclosure are the statutory requirements for investigators and prosecutors to disclose material that has been acquired during the investigation but is unused in the prosecution case. The logic is very straightforward in that if an investigator discovers evidence that is likely to support or corroborate a defence argument of innocence, then the police have a legal responsibility to disclose the material to the defendant and/or the defence lawyers. For instance, a number of recent serious rape trials have had to be abandoned because police and prosecutors failed to disclose information that supported the defence case that the sexual intercourse was consensual.

The problem is multi-faceted. The law that directs disclosure procedures was drafted and enacted prior to the common use of high capacity digital devices, such as internet connected mobile phones and tablets, where huge volumes of data can be stored. In the course of an investigation, if the police deem it necessary to analyse the content of, say, a mobile phone in order to explore for evidence of culpability, then they have a responsibility to search for evidence of innocence as well. If, for instance, there is reasonable suspicion that a phone contains social media exchanges relating to a victim's complaint of rape, then clearly this would be relevant for the prosecution as potentially corroborating an early complaint of the crime. There may similarly be a claim from the suspect that they exchanged explicit photographs on their phones and this may add to a defence case that the act was consensual. In both circumstances, the police must disclose their findings and, in the final judgment, it is a matter for the court to decide where the weight and truth of the total evidence lies. The substantial point is that searching for such evidence is hugely time consuming, which was not something anticipated by the legislation. It can be tempting, therefore, to truncate analysis once incriminating evidence has been discovered and move forward with the case, leaving potentially useful evidence undiscovered and undisclosed.

This problem is, however, not as new as might be imagined. Major fraud and economic crime investigations have historically failed due to problems of disclosure. For instance, the volume of paper-based records held by banks and insurance companies is massive and virtually impossible to search. Regrettably, police failure to select material from these sources that could potentially be of benefit to a defence case has resulted in acquittals at court. Similarly, e-mail exchanges over several years that might be surmised to be relevant in support of a particular position are tedious to recover, potentially without any confidence that the material will be of any value to either side. But nevertheless, if a witness in a case claims that an e-mail string supported a particular fact or issue, and then the work has to be tackled.

The problem with the disclosure regime is therefore straightforward in concept, but very much more complex, time consuming, and muddled in practicality. Added to which, the danger that investigators hold onto 'pet' theories as to the commission of a crime can prevent an officer from seeing or, much less, searching for evidence that contradicts the major lines of enquiry; a phenomena discussed earlier. There are, of course, potentially more mischievous reasons why disclosure can be an issue. An obvious example is the historical sexual activity of a rape complainant, which may or may not be relevant to a current allegation. The situation may be further complicated if a pregnancy is present. What the police disclose is therefore enormously controversial, but nevertheless it is unarguably essential to comply with the law. There is a clear case for a legal review of these issues and others and also a need to review the practicalities of the procedures, with a view to producing revised guidance for police and prosecutors.

The disclosure problems are not, however, totally beyond solution. Indeed, since the legislation was first introduced, there has been acknowledged 'best practice', which to a large extent solves some of the problems identified and contributes to the confidence of defence lawyers that all unused and relevant material has been made available. It is common practice in all major investigations to appoint one or more disclosure officers whose chief responsibility is to review all the evidence gathered by the investigation team in order to determine whether any discovery is relevant to a defence. The experience here, as touched upon earlier, is that there is a common temptation for investigators, and particularly senior investigating officers leading large teams, to be slow to move away from the crime and offender theories they have developed in respect of their case. There are even examples of cases where investigators have stubbornly adhered to their theories even in the face of corroborated evidence to the contrary! Hence the practical desirability of having a disclosure officer who is not a member of the operational investigation team, but slightly detached from it, and tasked to review material, including that which might not necessarily form a part of a prosecution case and may potentially be of value to a defence. In effect, such an appointment is acting as an agent for the defence and diligence applied to the role can make a significant contribution to a defence case. Indeed, it is not unusual for the police to receive glowing messages of thanks from defence lawyers at the conclusion of criminal trials, commending the officer(s) responsible for the disclosure function, whether or not there was an acquittal.

An essential feature of this work is the maintenance of a meticulous log of all the evidence, including witness statements, document seizures, forensic recovery, and of course the analytical product of the examination of digital devices, including CCTV recordings, whether digital or analogue. The police major incident enquiry computer systems have applications and routines for this process and providing the disclosure officer is appointed and is diligent, the final log is of considerable value to both the prosecutor and the defender. In fact, in some cases it has been found valuable to allocate a suitable room for the display of all the accumulated evidential material, with the associated log, and to provide access to defence lawyers and their representatives to review the material in their own time. Such a process is not only obviously valuable for a defence team, but it also helps to build confidence in the integrity of the police investigation, which can have a benefit during a trial process.

Another perhaps less obvious benefit of the role of the well trained disclosure officer is that the evidence is reviewed, as it is acquired, in an ongoing process, rather than waiting until the conclusion of the investigation and then retrospectively reviewing the material. The benefit will be clear in that it is more straightforward to understand the content and context of recovered material as it is acquired rather than to be confronted with a potentially enormous quantity of statements, documents, forensic reports, and analyses to review at the end of what could be a lengthy and protracted investigation. Even the most straightforward investigations have the potential to accumulate impressive quantities of data of all types and the more complex can result in many hundreds of thousands of pages, so tackling an ongoing disclosure function is essential, rather than desirable.

A damaging consequence of such an over-burdened, slow investigative prosecution and trial system is that that police are tempted to see disruption of criminal activities as preferable to prosecution. In such circumstances, instead of gathering evidence, officers may turn to intelligence gathering where the methods and standards of information acquisition may not be as high as when that information has to be tested as evidence. The information obtained, if it points towards a particular individual or group, may simply be used to prevent the crimes from continuing or recurring. In its most straightforward form, exposing what is known about their activities and warning about future conduct might simply achieve disruption of the activities of those concerned. This approach is not too distant from the method used by police to give warnings to individuals who promptly admit to low level crime. Here, of course, there is an official record. But where such methods are used without forming a part of the official cautioning system, the opportunities for corruption are increased, a topic that is addressed in Chapter Nine. At the more serious level, disruption of criminal activity in preference to criminal prosecution becomes a more significant concern. Police deciding for themselves which serious matters are prosecuted and which are not has in the past been a route to the corruption of officers involved.

The disruption of known criminal activities might be achieved through a range of both overt and covert means, but the outcomes are similar in that the current known criminality ceases or is displaced and the individuals concerned are, for the time being, dissuaded from continuing. This is not a tactic that is risk free, however. It sensitises criminals to police methods and intelligence sources, therefore it is likely to start off a hunt by the criminals for any suspected police informants and, most worryingly of all, it creates a situation in which the police alone become the arbiters of justice, rather than the systems and procedures set up for that purpose.

For these, and other obvious reasons, it is important to ensure there are an adequate number of trained investigators to carry out the necessary work to the standards required by the criminal justice system (CJS) and that they are effectively led. As has been shown, effective detectives do not grow on trees, neither are they born; they need careful selection, training, and exposure to appropriate experiences. It is undoubtedly one of those occupations that simply cannot be replicated outside professional policing, because the opportunities are not available elsewhere to provide the exposure to crime and criminals. However, exposure to crime and criminality brings with it further issues, in that it is imperative that such officers are provided with the leadership and support they need to retain their integrity and to be effective in the face of potentially corrupting influences; this is a topic which is further discussed in Chapter Nine.

In some other UK law enforcement organisations, lawyers,

accountants, and other professionals, including civil servants, who lead investigations and tackle the search for evidence do so in a markedly different way to trained police investigators. In such situations, investigations are frequently approached as intellectual exercises, whereby the circumstances are compared to available statutory provisions and evidence is accumulated and examined to reveal the best fit between the alleged criminal behaviour and the law. This is a fairly tedious way of approaching an investigation. A police approach would be to preserve all available evidence, either at the time or close to the time of report, and then search for the best evidence in support or refutation of the allegation; in other words, a search for the truth.

A criticism of this police approach might be that is has the potential to overlook associated and relevant material. It is, however, often too easy to be drawn away from the main lines of enquiry into what seems to be potentially relevant associated matters. Experience teaches that investigative terms of reference have to be tightly drawn in order for a serious and complex matter to be brought to any sort of conclusion and not to allow the investigation to endlessly continue pursuing trivial issues that are unlikely to be legally admissible, or be of any evidential value.

A trivial quip (favoured by police) that illustrates the difference in the police and non-police approaches is the solution to finding a needle in a haystack. A search by non-police investigators would start at the top right corner of the haystack and finish at the opposite, bottom left. A police detective would first seek witnesses and ask, "Who last saw the needle?"

This somewhat flippant comment does, however, conceal a

most important decision for any investigator and that is when and where it is chosen to question, or perhaps arrest a suspect? Many contemporary investigations are riddled with instances whereby detectives, for some apparently valid reason at the time, have either questioned or arrested their suspect too early in the investigative process, frequently revealing the lack of evidence they have to support a successful prosecution. In other words, the inexperienced detective will be relying on obtaining evidence from the suspect by way of interview, or by searching the suspect's accommodation and possessions in the hope of finding something incriminating. Clearly, if there is good reason to believe that a suspect is planning to travel away, then the best course might well be to pre-empt this by an early arrest. Similarly, in the case of a suspect found at the scene of a crime, the best course may be to arrest there and then if there is sufficient evidence. In most other cases, however, it is frequently to the advantage of a prosecution case to assemble sufficient evidence to prove the case before arresting the suspects. This tactic, in large part, removes the advantage a suspect might gain by only providing a 'no comment interview'. In such instances, where the detectives have sufficient evidence to proceed without any material contribution from the suspect, the advantage swings towards the prosecution who need only record any comments that are made, safe in the knowledge that they are able to move forward. The opposite is to engage in an evidential fishing trip that relies on questioning the suspect or searching the suspects' accommodation and possessions in the hope of finding something relevant and prejudicial. Of course, suspects have the right to remain silent if they wish and very often will be advised to remain so by defence lawyers. However, if this is a suspects' decision, having been correctly cautioned, the prosecution may comment on this and leave a court to infer the reason, which may often not be to the defendants' advantage when given the opportunity to offer explanation or mitigation.

That is not to say that a suspect should be denied the opportunity of giving an explanation, indeed quite the reverse. The problem with relying on interviews from a future defendant is that it will almost certainly be challenged by the defence. A suggestion often being that the defendant was put under pressure by the interviewing officer, or the circumstances under which the interview was conducted. Such as comments made before an interview, the presence of others prior to the interview, distractions, not understanding recording equipment, and other more obscure assertions. In short, if a prosecution is relying only on interview evidence, it will almost certainly fail and in fact is unlikely to be authorised by the CPS.

As with most decisions concerning investigative strategy, delaying the arrest of a suspect is not without risks. Evidence might degrade, or be destroyed, potential witnesses might be intimidated, and the suspect has an improved opportunity to construct an elaborate alibi. It may thus be appreciated that the timing of an arrest is an important consideration for investigators and should not be taken lightly, but preferably after careful consideration with experienced case supervisors. From the suspects' point of view, an early arrest can frequently be followed by a long period of police bail or release from custody pending further enquiries. This can be hugely damaging to innocent individuals, sometimes resulting in suspension from their work, fractured family relationships, and medical problems. In extreme cases, self-harm and suicide attempts occur. The majority of which might be avoided by thoughtful consideration not only of the investigation itself, but also of the context of the allegations and the individual suspects concerned. Regrettably, too often the police and others use powers that are excessive and disproportionate to the objectives, typically arrest, search, and detention, when other alternatives are available. A power of arrest is just one of several means of making a person amenable to justice and should be exercised with great care, especially in such circumstances as described above and where there is no likelihood of the alleged offence being repeated or continuing. For instance, where a person is suspected of a minor and non-violent offence that is not suitable for a police caution, where the home address is verified and, for pressing family reasons, he or she is unlikely to abscond, it may well be appropriate to summons a person to appear before a court rather than to arrest. Simply, because a legal power exists, it does not mean it has to be used in all cases.

A typical and frequently used police tactic that illustrates this point is the early morning surprise arrest at a person's residence. In such circumstances, the suspect will often be woken, arrested, instructed to dress, and conveyed to a custody suite after the home and personal possessions have been thoroughly searched and possibly seized. The principal police justification for such practices is that it prevents destruction of evidence and the element of surprise minimises the potential for a violent confrontation and the construction of an alibi. Such methods, however, are usually wholly disproportionate in all but the most serious cases when the suspect is a known and experienced criminal. The arrest of individuals in this way is an intrusive and traumatic experience, which should be confined to investigations where the justification is clear and not imaginary. Such actions can have a long lasting and negative impact on a suspect, his or her family, neighbours, and others who will see the police as heavy handed, regardless of the suspect's culpability.

The skilled and experienced investigator will avoid such mistakes because they can give a prosecution a very negative image and such instances might be cited in court as evidence of overbearing conduct by the police, which is unlikely to find favour with judges or juries. It seems that, in certain circumstances, often driven and exacerbated by the media, the police find themselves driven to what can only be described as overzealous investigations, so they can clearly be seen to be reacting robustly. Such temptations must be resisted and it is a priority for police leaders to use their experience to ensure that investigative teams always behave in a proportionate and moderate way. Anything else will be seen as overbearing and, as already remarked on, can result in very negative consequences for a prosecution.

A further extension of this tendency for the police to over react to allegations has arisen from the quite shocking testimonies of young people who have been victims of sexual offences. It is doubtful whether any sensible and mature person would be anything other than deeply shocked by some of these revelations and this, of course, also has an impact on the police. It has been seen that the police become galvanised into action, stimulated by the media, and desperate to be seen to be responding as they perceive most of the public would wish. In doing so, proportionality occasionally flies away and robust tactics are deployed from the start. Major searches of homes and possessions by numerous officers, public appeals for witnesses, intrusive surveillance, and high profile arrests are just some of the very visible tactics that police can deploy to demonstrate that they are taking matters seriously. However, in all the flurry of being seen to be doing the right thing, very often the testing of the original allegations is overlooked. Indeed, current directions to the police require that allegations of sexual crimes should be accepted at face value and be treated as truthful. Experience, however, teaches that people make allegations of crime for a variety of reasons and sometimes those people are close to the police for other reasons. For instance, they may be a registered police informant, or someone who routinely has contact with the police in either an official or a social context. It becomes relatively straightforward to then make allegations of crime against another who they wish to see suffer, or be punished in some way. At a fairly low level of criminal behaviour, this often manifests through neighbour disputes over noise, pets, trees, fences, and so on, where one protagonist exaggerates the degree of nuisance in the hope that the police will take some enforcement action. More seriously, though, an allegation of sexual misconduct by a prominent public figure will potentially have a devastating impact on that individuals' reputation, whether or not he or she is ever convicted of a crime. So, for the police to overreact to such allegations is clearly inappropriate. Rather, the allegations should be tested for accuracy before an intrusive investigation is launched. Such a 'scoping' investigation is usually best undertaken covertly or at least discreetly. The motive of an individual making the allegations can be explored and some initial testing of the allegations made, usually involving checking dates, time, locations, capability, etc. of the accuser and the suspect. In this way, the police can very quickly arrive at a view as to whether the allegation is being made for mischievous reasons, or whether a crime or crimes have indeed been committed. Such an approach also has the benefit of identifying whether there is any likelihood of adequate evidence being available to support a prosecution, and if so, from where it might be obtained. The danger of just accepting the un-tested reliability of serious victim allegations is well known to police. Certainly, for many years it was common to treat rape allegations with a huge degree of scepticism, especially where the victim knew the alleged perpetrator and they had been together in a social setting. However, quite rightly, more recent policy has been to accept such allegation as substantive, unless evidence arises to the contrary, so the cynical police officers' view, that the victim consented but has regretted her behaviour with hindsight, is no longer a police mindset. Similarly, many police officers are experienced at dis-entangling the mixed motives of criminal informants, many of whom make all sorts of allegations about other criminals for their own purposes and also against police officers, with a view to damaging reputations. So, testing allegations is not a new skill set, but one that seems to have fallen from favour. This may be partly due to policy guidance from Her Majesty's Chief Inspector of Constabulary (the former HMCIC), who quite properly has directed that all allegations of sexual crime should be recorded as such. This really should not have been an issue that needed clarification for police, it is a simple matter of making an initial crime record and registering the allegation in the official recording system. There is nothing in the policy that directs that if the allegation is subsequently shown to be mischievous or vexatious, then the statistical record can be amended to show a more accurate record. Such a policy is clearly not intended to prevent police officers from keeping an open mind about the truth of what they are being told by anyone; victims, suspects, or witnesses.

Regrettably, though, the pool of skilled investigators who have the experience and the curiosity to unravel some of these more complex matters is really quite limited in each of the public, private, and commercial sectors. Those who are working in the private sector generally have civilian or military police backgrounds, with a limited few having intelligence service or similar experience. The difficulty they face, though, in acquiring appropriate skills and experience simply comes from the commercial pressures to sustain the commercial business, not to become a second tier law enforcement organisation. Therefore, private sector investigations invariably stop short of criminal prosecution simply because it is not in the businesses' (or organisations') interests to carry a case on to court. Potential business reputational damage, a lack of total confidence in the evidence, no guarantees of winning, and the likely consequential direct costs are all sufficient reasons not to press ahead with a prosecution. Therefore, the investigators, who may have done an excellent job up to the point of a decision to withdraw, have little opportunity to test their work in the courts. The decision to 'let someone go' on the basis of a partial or incomplete investigation is therefore very often the outcome of a business' internal crime allegation.

As already noted, one of the hardest decisions in police work is deciding when to scale down an investigation because there is no realistic prospect of securing the necessary evidence. It is intensely frustrating to know that a guilty person has, for the time being, escaped justice and that victims have been denied their justice, too. However, in resource terms, it is invariably necessary to re-direct investigators to the next crime allegation as time is often crucial to the acquisition of evidence.

Indeed, many experienced detectives refer to the so-called 'golden hour', or the period following the commission of a crime when the best opportunity is presented to secure evidence. Failure to allocate adequate resources to an investigation during this period is often an omission that results in failure. Of course, it is a difficult decision to divert detectives from one case to another, often with very short notice, but the opportunity for the loss of evidence after an hour or so is a very real prospect. Weather can destroy forensic opportunities, as can road traffic, witnesses carry on their way, or cannot recall a significant detail, suspects and accomplices have the opportunity to arrange alibis, and so on. So, it is really important to grasp the opportunities of the 'golden hour'.

From a police leadership perspective, the golden hour also presents a number of challenges in that not only must adequate resources be assigned, but as importantly, staff with appropriate skills and experience. Critical and serious incidents have an almost predictable, common characteristic in that they invariably occur at times and in places that do not conveniently correspond with staff availability. Effectively, this means that even in the largest police organisations, the most suitable officers and staff to take on particular roles will be unavailable for unavoidable reasons. Typically, being away from work during the night, weekends, on holiday, or absent for some other reason. Inevitably, therefore, that when senior leaders are (hopefully?) informed of a serious or critical incident, the most appropriate person to lead the golden hour opportunities will not be present. This then becomes a test of leadership, as endeavouring to advise and direct operations from a distance, at the end of a radio or telephone, is hardly the most effective way to ensure that matters are handled swiftly and effectively.

Neither is it the best method to quickly assimilate the scope, seriousness, and complexity of the incident. In many such circumstances, senior leaders will simply not be convinced that the best outcomes will be achieved without their personal presence and quite rightly make the decision to attend the crime scene. Similarly, when a leader knows that the skills and experience are just not present, then alternative solutions have to be organised; other officers with appropriate skills have to be contacted and called out. The challenge is, of course, having sufficient knowledge of, and trust in, those individuals who are available to deal with the incident. The implication, of course, being that senior police operational leaders, typically, assistant chief constables and commanders, must have a personal knowledge of the strengths and limitations of the operational teams under their command. This necessity underlines the importance of senior officers being operationally competent themselves and well known to their staff as individuals who engage with operational problems and service delivery at all levels; this reputation cannot be achieved from behind a desk at police headquarters.

In order to be able to add value to the work of officers responding to a serious or critical incident, it is necessary for senior leaders to be able to ask appropriate questions in order to illicit responses that will enable them to direct, advise, and encourage. Without this ability, it will quickly become apparent to all involved that the senior intervention is not adding benefit, indeed probably the opposite.

It may be appreciated, from this description of criminal casework and operational management, that police are locked into an ever ascending spiral of demands, much as modelled by the NP 'reactive loop'. However, the NP thesis emphasised the importance of preventive measures in police work in order to moderate the demand spiral affect and it is in this regard that experienced detectives make a significant impact.

The use of criminal intelligence has increased significantly during the past few decades. During the 1960's and early 1970's, the function of gathering, storing, and retrieving information relating to crimes and criminals was a fairly low priority. Detectives in the main relied on their own criminal informants and jealously guarded their identity. Information coming from such sources was frequently unreliable, often being motivated by greed, revenge, jealousy, family loyalties, and so forth, most of which were untestable by the police officer receiving the information. The use of disciplined and regulated intelligence systems was not, therefore, generally highly regarded and certainly not a great deal of effort was put into the development of such systems for policing purposes. However, this situation was later to change very quickly and very effectively.

One of the attributes of an effective detective has been, and continues to be, a refined knowledge of who is actively committing crime in a particular locality, or who has the ability and motivation to commit particular types of crime, such as armed robbery, fraud, sexual offences, and so on. Sophisticated intelligence storage, retrieval, and analytical systems now have the capability to supplement the detectives' local knowledge and which can support potentially very helpful theories about who is, and who will be committing crime, where, and when. For instance, it is widely known by criminologists that a relatively few recidivist criminals commit the vast majority of crime. Local intelligence systems have the capability of identifying such individuals and providing information about their criminal habits. Local and regional prioritisation of which particular criminal will become subject to the attention of detectives is a common and effective practice. Such targeting enables police to gather evidence in support of prosecuting these recidivist individuals, thus at least preventing further crimes for the duration of their imprisonment.

There is no doubt that such methods can be most effective, if diligently supervised, but it is important for police managers to strictly control target identification and the tactics that are used for intelligence acquisition. The hopefully isolated practice of individual police officers deciding who should be pursued, and by what means, is a short route to potentially overbearing and corrupt practices and should never occur; effective supervision is essential here. Despite the obvious risks of targeting recidivist criminals, there are clear benefits to the tactic in terms of crime prevention, thus potentially easing the tension within the police demand spiral and providing the public with a greater degree of reassurance that persistent criminality is being tackled.

Regrettably, though, the means by which this reassurance was largely attempted during the 1980's and 1990's was through a number of publicity-led campaigns aimed at particular types of crime, for instance street robberies, residential burglaries, car crime, and similar definable categories of crime. The aim was to heighten public awareness of a particular type of crime and to associate this with encouragement of the public to implement preventive measures. For instance, physical security measures applied to homes, property marking schemes, and various other gadgets to deter criminals, such as personal attack alarms. Meanwhile, so the thinking went, the police would focus their attention on solving the types of crime specified in the publicity. It should have been quite clear at the outset that such initiatives would fail in almost every respect, apart from filling media space and time with police publicity. Subsequently, the public acquired a particularly unhealthy fear of crime, especially from older people who feared burglary of their homes and younger people who were the regular users of urban streets at night, which they perceived to be threatening. Of course, the recidivist criminals, who also absorbed the police propaganda, simply found new criminal opportunities and/or displaced their activities to areas where police attention was less intense. The effect was that the incidence of other acquisitive crimes came to the fore. Retail thefts became more organised, metal and agricultural crime were a popular and less risky activity, crimes associated with the sex trade, people trafficking, and, of course, dealing in prohibited drugs all showed increases during this time. These police tactics were inevitably to fail as the motivation of persistent criminals was not factored into the operations. Had the lifestyle of the career criminal been taken into account, then these operations would have relied less on publicity and more on intelligence-led operations, which of course are now common police practice.

Police intelligence operations can be personally and professionally challenging to those involved and the close supervision of such operations is essential in order to prevent excesses occurring, but none more so than in the deployment of covert acquisition methods. Intrusive information gathering by means of telephone intercepts, covert CCTV, or the introduction of an undercover police officer, are all activities regulated by statute and require the authority of senior police officers, and in the more serious matters, that of the Home Secretary. Before any such methods are considered, it must be established whether alternative methods are likely to produce similar information. If covert methods are used, however, despite the level of the authority required for an operation, which by definition is an invasion of someone's privacy, the degree of management attention that is given to the operation is likely to be the indicator of success. Some recent high profile cases have sadly revealed how easy it is for officers employed on such covert tasks to exceed the boundaries of either the law or good practice, by a fixation on revealing information that they consider to be of value. The pursuit of such information is not something that is to be achieved at all costs and covert activities must be regularly reviewed for compliance with the original authority and whether the continued deployment of such tactics is likely to produce a worthwhile outcome. Intelligence 'fishing trips' by covert means are just not good practice and any information gained by such tactics is unlikely to have any reliable intelligence use or, much less, any evidential value.

The same 'health warning' applies to information gained by the analysis of mobile phone data, hand held cameras, CCTV systems, computers, and any other electronic device that stores information. Clearly, the acquisition by police of CCTV data from security cameras in town centres, shopping malls, and similar public places is of great value when investigating crimes occurring in these locations. CCTV is very often the first material to provide any reliable information about what exactly occurred and it also may have a significant evidential value, either for a prosecution or defence. In contrast, however, when it comes to police attention that computers, smart phones, and similar devices are relevant to a particular crime, it becomes more important to limit the scope of the analysis of these devices to the specific interest of the investigation at that time. Here again, explorative data fishing trips, which are not underpinned by a recorded, reasonable suspicion of what might be contained in the device, are likely to be of little intelligence value and almost certainly of little evidential value. However, as discussed earlier, it is important in such circumstances to disclose the scope of the data analysis that has been undertaken to the defence as an element of the disclosure process. If it is considered that further analysis of a device would reveal material relevant to a suspect's defence, then the police must expand their efforts to embrace this possibility and disclose the scope of the examination.

The law, it seems, is quite clear in this respect. The Human Rights Act provides everyone with the right to a respect for his or her privacy, family life, home, and correspondence. There shall be no interference with this right except as provided by law, where it is necessary in the interests of national security, public safety, the country's economic wellbeing, the prevention of crime or disorder, the protection of health or morals, or for the protection of the rights of others. There are a number of statutory provisions that give police the powers to interfere with this right to privacy, but in all matters, the interference must be proportionate and designed to meet the objective in question; it must not be arbitrary or unfair. In any event, evidence which has been obtained outside the detail of these provisions would almost certainly be inadmissible in any criminal proceedings. It is also noteworthy that the law places a requirement on investigators to retain any information obtained from such sources, which might be relevant to a particular case, for revelation to the defence.

One of the primary drivers of the use of forensic evidence

gained from electronic devices, including mobile phones, DNA profiling, ballistics analysis, and other similar and laboratory-based testing, is the demonstrable unreliability of much witness evidence. It is certainly not unusual for witnesses to a particular crime to alter their story under examination in a witness box. This may not necessarily be a deliberate attempt to vary their account of events for a cynical motive, but a genuine belief that they now don't believe what they actually witnessed and the way they described events to police at the time. Similarly, witnesses often become confused as to what and who they saw, and where. Again, this may not be a deliberate ploy to, say, bolster the prosecution case, or strengthen the defence arguments, merely a genuine mistake. Occasionally, over enthusiastic prosecutors and counsel will bully witnesses in court in an attempt to cast doubt on their account and to reveal weakness in their testimony. However, it is the responsibility of the presiding judge or magistrate to prevent this from occurring and to allow the reliability of witnesses' accounts to be assessed by juries or magistrates. The reality is that these witness frailties are evidently sufficiently frequent to have encouraged investigators to attach great importance to forensic recovery from crime scenes and thus to be able to provide courts with evidence that is more reliable and less susceptible to challenge. It is not surprising, therefore, that criminal investigations now frequently rely on forensic evidence as the principal means of establishing the truth.

This trend in itself has led to the emergence of further problems for investigators and in particular those who prosecute criminal cases. Frequently, forensic analysis relies upon multiple statistical probabilities that can present fairly significant challenges to clear understanding. Those presenting cases have to find ways of encouraging scientists, who provide the results, to do so in ways that are comprehensible to juries and magistrates who may not necessarily be highly numerate, or familiar with conceptual statistics. The obvious example here is the growth in the use of DNA profiling in criminal cases, usually involving a comparison between a sample from the scene or the victim and the defendant. The degree of certainty (or probability) that can be given to a particular match is almost entirely derived from the processing power of the computers used, in conjunction with the statistical algorithms that are relied upon for the analysis. The complexity increases very quickly as this topic is explored and understandably, and frequently, becomes difficult to present to non-scientists. Despite this limitation, though, the use of DNA profiling has enabled investigators to bring forward cases that would otherwise have been incapable of successful prosecution. Doubtless, in the future, courts will become more willing to accept more visual presentations of complex evidence, rather than just relying on the aural accounts and explanations of witnesses in person.

The mid 1980's saw the creation of the Crown Prosecution Service (CPS), the principal function of which was to consider the evidence in more serious cases before making a decision as to whether to charge the suspect that the police investigation had identified. Hitherto, such decisions had been taken by the police themselves, usually by a comparatively junior officer, typically the station sergeant, whose job it was to review the facts of the case as presented by the investigating officer and to decide upon the charge, which had most often been prepared by the investigators in advance. The major problem with this system is that simply neither the content, nor the integrity of the evidence, could be properly tested before a suspect had to appear in court. Hardly a fair system for the accused, who had been put into that situation by the police alone, without any independent oversight of the correctness of procedures, merit of the case, the strength of the evidence, or the public interest. This situation inevitably led to frequent accusations that the police had fabricated evidence, accepted inducements to release suspects, or 'not find' relevant and discoverable evidence. The CPS was, therefore, a major step forward in ensuring the propriety of the criminal prosecution process. It also meant that investigators had to be far more assiduous in their acquisition, preparation, and accumulation of evidence to submit to the CPS. Previously, detectives might form the view that a particular suspect was guilty of a particular crime and the individual in question would be charged on the basis of minimal evidence. The detectives would then use the period between charging and the first appearance in court to obtain any corroborative, or supplementary evidence. Quite rightly, this all had to stop with the implementation of the functions of the CPS, who would insist that the full case file of evidence was available before a decision was made to charge a suspect, thus providing much needed safeguards and bringing UK justice into line with other jurisdictions. This move clearly had the outcome of professionalising criminal investigations and bringing a scrutiny to cases that had been absent hitherto.

Considerations regarding the adequacy of evidence went alongside the concept of whether a prosecution would be in the public interest. The consequence of this was that police detectives had to become used to working with criminal lawyers much more closely than had been the case previously, when private or employed solicitors were instructed by the police to bring forward a case for prosecution almost regardless of its merits. Clearly, investigations now took much longer, but did at least arrive at court with some expectation of success, rather than the earlier approaches to run a case with whatever evidence was available and hope for a sympathetic jury.

The CPS was not without problems for police, however. Whilst benefits accrued to the criminal justice system generally, police experienced an equal, but opposite effect, in that the CPS effectively became an intermediate, judicial layer between the courts and the police; another hurdle to overcome to achieve justice. Frequently, investigators were being faced with having to make explanations to victims as to why matters were not being taken forward as they expected. It was not very long before the reputation of the CPS became one of risk aversion, bureaucracy, and often carelessness, which developed into a culture typified by delay, prevarication, and an absence of any consideration for victims and witnesses. In short, the CPS was not seen as a *prosecution* service, but rather a pre-trial impediment to justice. It must be said that this somewhat extreme view was not confined to the police and was shared by many criminal lawyers in private practice, magistrates, and members of the judiciary. It is, of course, appropriate to note that not all regional CPS branches functioned in exactly the same way, but the overall situation was never especially positive as far as the police were concerned. Now, however, relationships and procedures are very much improved, but the CPS are nevertheless responsible for making decisions about prosecutions based on their assessment of the likelihood of success, weighed against the cost. This approach can all too often result in lesser charges being brought than are implied by the circumstances of the crime and the allegation of the victim.

The consequence for police detectives moral is all too often very negative.

A system, which has been shown to be effective, that goes a long way to solving these problems on a routine basis is the provision of a twenty-four-hour CPS office within the busier police custody suites. Here, CPS lawyers are available to advise on the progress of an investigation from the earliest stage after a suspect has been arrested. The benefits are considerable; police have a closer and more productive relationship with the lawyers, the CPS staff are frequently engaged with witnesses and victims, the opportunity is present for the police to be quickly advised as to necessary further evidence, leading to an appropriate and potentially successfully prosecuted charge. Paradoxically, both police and the CPS have resisted such experiments. The police claiming a further erosion of their primary role to investigate and arrest and the CPS claiming a loss of independence and thus a diminution of their responsibilities. Here again it seems the losers will be the victims if these tendencies are not resisted. The comparatively new initiative of 'CPS Direct' certainly offers some opportunity for greater telephone access by police to CPS advice on a twenty-four-hour basis, but it is not clear how successful the scheme is for the police.

Fortunately, such problems are not apparent in regard to the more lengthy and serious matters, where specialist police investigators work very closely with specialist sections of the CPS to build cases. Frequently, where leading counsel are to be instructed to present serious cases in court, counsel will be identified by the CPS and involved in pre-trial conferences with the CPS and the police. Although there is a reluctance by the CPS to pay counsel's fees for such conferences, very often these independent advocates will not charge for their time as they see it as highly beneficial to case preparation. The outcome is invariably successful, due to the close understanding that is developed across the prosecution team.

The most effective way forward must be for more collaboration between police and prosecutors. Notions of independence, which leads to isolation and separation between the component organisations of the criminal justice, will never allow the full potential of professional competencies to be realised by working together for a common outcome. It would be quite feasible to reduce delays in the criminal justice system if these improvements were to be made. Greater use of overnight detention of suspects, with longer court sittings, especially during evenings and weekends, would be a most positive step in administering effective justice. Of course, such moves would be far from popular for all and probably with the legal practitioners with family responsibilities who have become used to a day time work routine. However, if the larger and more pressing problem is to improve investigative speed and effectiveness, whilst avoiding dramatically increasing expenditure, then greater collaboration across the elements of the criminal justice system is an obvious starting point.

Such cross fertilisation and appreciation of complimentary professional skills and capabilities would be a fairly straightforward programme to introduce. The Department of Justice would be a good starting point and, of course, the Home Office could provide police officers at all levels with insight into some of the problems of administering the criminal justice system. It remains to be seen whether civil servants will ever be seen working a night duty on a Saturday in a major urban conurbation, or patrolling a remote rural area where the availability of 'back up' is just an interesting concept, rather than a reality.

In order to consolidate this greater degree of collaboration, and following earlier discussion (Chapter Two), there should be no reason, given that other personal attributes are present, why a CPS lawyer should not be able to enhance his or her career by a period employed as a police detective, to return to legal practice at a mutually convenient point. Similarly, given that a police officer is professionally qualified to practice as a lawyer, a period as a prosecutor would be a positive advantage to a police career. Of course, this will never be possible, as already discussed, if Police Regulations in relation to salaries and terms and conditions of police employment are as restrictive as they are at present.

One factor that should be apparent from the discussion in this chapter is that police operations and investigations are challenging for those involved, challenging to lead, and invariably subject to critical analysis, with the benefit of hindsight, by politicians, the media, the courts, and others. This means that in order to deliver a consistently improving service, the police must be alert to the changes necessary, both within police organisations as well as others associated services, and be active in promoting movement in opinions to bring about necessary changes. To stubbornly rely on established traditions in this essential public service is almost certainly a strategy for failure.

Chapter Ten addresses this question of designing and implementing change in police organisations.

7.

Measuring Policing

The Statistics Games

A little harsh, perhaps, but in this chapter the importance of quantification of police activity is discussed and how such information might be used to enhance efficiency and effectiveness. Some fresh approaches and refinements to established measurement methods are proposed, together with some propositions for future trials.

The provision of quantification of organisational functioning and output are essential tools for anyone who is managing either a public or private sector organisation. Despite an apparently declining enthusiasm amongst the population generally for numbers, arithmetic, statistics, and mathematics, there is no doubting the importance of figures and numeracy to organisational functioning. It is simply not possible to assess either the internal functioning, or the output performance of an organisation, without a regular and comparable stream of data that illustrates the critical aspects of the business, whether it is profit making, charitable, or public service. It is, however, not unreasonable to suggest that in some instances this need for numbers can become obsessive. It is apparent that some businesses are managed so tightly on unit profit targets, that many other quantifiable activities, which are just as significant to good business health, are ignored in favour of a single indicator of success or failure. Some might argue that to concentrate management attention on a single numeric indicator is the best way to encourage staff to share a common objective, but such a narrow scope of evaluation will inevitably miss other success factors in the organisation. Conversely, multiple numeric indicators might be contradictory, or difficult to assimilate, and add confusion rather than clarity to understanding an organisation's performance. Disentangling a plethora of numbers can be a challenging experience for even the most numerate manager, without the advantage of some analysis supplied by the relevant functional professional. For instance, financial reports that provide a surfeit of data without any interpretation are useless to a board. Executive time spent trying to unravel such data is not time well spent and therefore the qualitative supplement provided by a financial specialist is essential to a complete understanding of the material presented.

The same is true for any data that purports to represent the activities of organisations' outputs or activities. If the data is not analysed and supplemented by a qualitative and contextual commentary from an individual who understands the processes and procedures that are subject of the data, then the information will be useless at worst, or misleading at best. However, this does not diminish the importance of having access to quantification of organisations' functioning and policing is no exception.

The measurement of demands on police, and the responses made, is essential to the proper functioning of police organisations and the optimal deployment of resources. Simple counting of reported crimes, traffic collisions, and other requests for assistance will reveal patterns that might be used to allocate staff to priorities. Further information regarding day, date, time, and location will then allow patrol deployment decisions to be made with more accuracy. Similarly, if a disproportionately high number of traffic collisions occur around the same time and at the same location, further questions and examinations can be made to determine the reason. There is nothing surprising here, traffic collision analysis has been a feature of road safety efforts for some years and, in particular, in order to identify locations where collisions are more frequent so that design and engineering solutions might be identified.

Information regarding the outcomes of reports in respect of other activities will enable judgements to be made about the performance of the police. For instance, the number of crimes detected as a proportion of the number reported will give some insight to efficiency. Further detail regarding specific crime types is, however, potentially more useful, in that comparisons can be made with successes, or not, in relation to other crime types. So, for instance, a good performance against, say, residential burglary, contrasting with a poor performance against crimes of violence, would surely prompt questions in the minds of police leaders and supervisors. Rape, for example, is a crime where the offender is frequently known to the victim, but typically has a very low conviction rate. A police leader giving full attention to such data would question why that is the case. It is worth mentioning in this connection that police leaders must be diligent in their oversight of specialist investigation units, including those tackling crimes such as rape. There has been a tendency for such specialist branches to decline to accept some crimes that specifically accord with their specialisation, but where the prospect of successful detections is seen as very unlikely. Such allegations, which if accepted for investigation, could, of course, have the effect of reducing the clear-up rate for the specialist branch, therefore potentially casting doubt over their claimed specialist expertise.

The use of descriptive statistics of police recorded events is very straightforward, but serves to illustrate how even the most basic data might be used to inform important decisions. The details of all crimes and collisions resulting in personal injury reported to the police are collected and stored according to a national standard. This makes comparisons between different police forces, in respect of some quite fine detail, a statistically reliable and intelligible matter. The problem being, of course, that viewed from a national level, such comparisons do not have the benefit of qualitative, supplementary information that is specific to a particular area or region, which might be highly significant to a particular comparison.

Notwithstanding the obvious limitations of presenting such highly aggregated data, the Home Office annually publishes recorded crime statistics and uses these as a means of comparing police force efficiency without this necessary qualification. It is tempting to suggest that even if appropriate qualification was supplied, it would be largely ignored by the media, who find more interest in an over-simplified, sensational statistic than something that is more thorough and thoughtful. There is also a hunger for reported crime statistics at local levels. Until comparatively recently, Police Authorities would routinely be presented with such material by the police, usually in an un-analysed form, on a month by month basis. Here again, the interest would frequently be in the headline figures; crime recording rate, is it up or down?; clear-up rate, is it up or down? Doubtless, the replacement Police and Crime Commissioners (PCCs) will be provided with similar information, which at the usual high level of aggregation is not especially informative. They will have a responsibility to demonstrate that they are handling their responsibilities rigorously and will probably use such data in support of their arguments to tax payers. It is not until local police engage with the detail of such recorded crime data that any real value might be drawn from the numbers.

Generally speaking, operational detectives are not too concerned with the detail of recorded crime numbers and are not trained to exploit such data, that is not what they joined the police to concentrate on. However, those that do take the time to understand the crime pictures and patterns behind the numbers are undoubtedly more successful in their work.

In a similar vein, much information can be drawn from the recording systems in use in police control rooms, where calls are received from the public for police attention, which may not be recordable crimes. It is a straightforward matter to extract information about the number of calls, in any given period, from any specified particular area, in relation to any specified call category, such as domestic disputes, other disturbances, and calls for assistance. Such data, if analysed by officers who have local knowledge and interest, can yield important information that is essential to patrol deployments and preventive activities; but held at central level and presented in an aggregate form, practically useless. Yet irrelevant and hugely misleading information, such as aggregate police response times, has been routinely retrieved from such systems and presented at government level. Worse still, comparisons have then been made between different police organisations; a classic statistical error of comparing apples with oranges.

The Neighbourhood Policing trials (1982) in the Metropolitan and Surrey Police areas, mentioned earlier, attempted to exploit relatively simple police 'demand' data with a view to informing police deployments. Data was collected regarding calls for police attendance and crimes by geographic location, time of day, and day of the week. Initially, the data was plotted manually, as the availability of suitable computing assistance was very limited. However, even by manual means, it was possible to quickly establish the areas and times of greatest demand and to deploy resources accordingly. In truth, however, a legitimate critique of this approach was that it added little fresh information to what local officers knew already to be the situation. It did seem somewhat problematic, though, that if this information was already to hand, or at least widely appreciated, why patrols did not follow the known patterns. Given the current easily acquired facilities of computerised, spacial plotting, with sophisticated graphical software, it is surprising more use is not made of this readily available demand data. It would be quite straightforward to provide a far more comprehensive picture of both routine demands, as well as attempting to develop forecasts. Other readily available data sets could be added to give a richer picture, such as demographics, entertainment and licensing data, tourist, transport, social, sporting, health care, and a range of other publicly available data, which would enhance the police demand profile for any given time or day. Police deployments could thus be made with more precision, rather than the traditional and administratively convenient approach.

With the clear brief to focus police attention on community priorities, PCCs will doubtless jump at the opportunity of utilising this readily available data to either review the effectiveness of the police, or to demonstrate to communities that their concerns have been addressed. Either way, it will be essential that the data is properly understood and presented with appropriate qualification. Giving into the temptation to over simplify the numbers and then to have them used as either a means to criticise the police, or to celebrate the success of the PCC, will be as discreditable as the previous inappropriate uses.

A particularly unproductive use of police data, which thankfully has now lost fashion, at least at national level, was the excessive and burdensome target setting regime introduced during the 1990's. Somebody in government must have read a book on management methods and concluded that 'what gets measured, gets done'. There followed a plethora of numerical targets for operational activities, most of which were outside the influence of police and many of which were impossible to achieve, even if police might have been able to affect outcomes. This did not stop, however, the annual scrutiny of the data by the Home Office inspectors, most of whom had little relevant operational experience and even less interest in anything other than the simple achievement or otherwise of these arbitrary targets. Targets, such as clear-up rates for specific crime types, were completely unreasonable, as the issues that defined whether a crime had been cleared up or not were largely outside the influence of police, including the public's propensity to report particular crimes. Similarly, the incidence of 'perverse incentives' stimulated by inappropriate targets became a regularly encountered phenomena. A situation was created whereby officers would be judged by their achievement of particular targets and would diligently concentrate on this, but what was being measured was not either what was important, or worthwhile, thus creating the perverse incentive. For instance, measuring response times from police receipt of a call from the public to the time of arrival of the police created a situation where excessive speeds were used for non-emergency calls, often resulting in avoidable collisions, injuries, or worse.

Many targets that were of relevance to the management of police organisations, such as the average number of self-certified sickness days per officer/year, were largely ignored by government inspectors. It is tempting to suggest that this was probably due to the very much more favourable rate of police absence when compared with other areas of the public sector. It is regrettable that target setting as a management tool has become largely discredited in much of policing, having been used as a very blunt instrument. There is no doubt, however, that used thoughtfully, achievement of agreed targets could be very satisfying for those concerned and very productive in terms of improving organisational efficiency.

Similarly, the use of performance indicators as a management tool has considerable potential benefits, but only if the temptation is resisted to have performance data on too many topics. Performance indicators are simply an expression of the unit of some activity expressed in relation to another variable. For instance, distance travelled per hour, investigations concluded per officer month, dog foot patrols per month, and many more. The danger here is that, whilst performance might be improved in respect of one function, it might be at cost of declining performance in another, a so-called zero sum game, so these indicators have to be selected with some care. Where there is a possibility of improvements only being achieved at the cost of another, then complimentary measures of both activities should be put in place to assess the benefits or otherwise of each. Only then will it be possible for the data to inform an objective decision as to which provides the most effective return and therefore which should take priority in the light of the organisation's ambitions.

The use of performance indicators will be especially important in the regime created around PCCs. These individuals are responsible for financial budgeting and performance indicators, which do provide the most straightforward means of determining whether the application of increased resources to a particular function proportionately improves performance or output. For instance, if uniform foot patrols in a city centre are increased by fifty percent between ten p.m. and two a.m. on Saturday evenings, is there a commensurate fall in the incidence of anti-social behaviour reports? If so, does the scale of the reduction warrant the increased cost, or are the problems merely displaced elsewhere? Provided rigorous measurement systems are put in place, the answers to such questions may be achieved relatively easily and reliably. However, it is not necessary to set up such data capture procedures and to leave them in place for any longer than necessary to answer the question. As soon as the cost of capturing and analysing data becomes greater than the value of the savings arising from the knowledge obtained, then it is time to seriously consider whether attention should be focused on something else.

It is important to reiterate here that, if such sampling methods and small scale evaluations are to be utilised, it is most important to ensure that both statistical validity and reliability are tested. Simply, is the data that is being captured actually measuring the activity of interest and can similar data capture exercises be repeated in the future? It is also important that such comparisons are made without confounding factors arising between measurements, distorting the results. If as a result of an exercise, such as the example given earlier, permanent changes are made to Saturday night deployments, but after several months, incidents return to the previous level, then it might become necessary to repeat the data exercise. Clearly, little will be gained from this approach if the results from the two evaluations differ due to methodological variations, therefore becoming incomparable.

These basic statistical concepts are as important in assessing policing functions as in any other, and yet they seem to be completely overlooked in many important topics. For instance, the police powers of 'stop and search' have been a continual source of disagreement between the police, government, and some minority ethnic communities for several decades. Simply expressed, the police consider stopping and searching people whom they reasonably suspect of having committed a criminal offence, or being about to commit a criminal offence, as a necessary detection and prevention tactic. Typically, the carrying of offensive weapons, illegal drugs, stolen mobile phones, etc. will be revealed by this tactic. Many individuals who are the subject of this tactic are young men from visible minority ethnic groups who claim they are disproportionately targeted by the police using these powers. A general claim is that they are required to submit to search procedures only because of their skin colour and alleged racist tendencies of police. Various attempts have been made by governments to establish the truth of both arguments, including an overly burdensome, paper-based recording system of all such stops and searches, which included the recording of a racial identity code. Conclusions were then drawn on the basis of comparing the proportions of visible minority ethnic men with that of white men who had been stopped and searched. Analysts concluded that, in many circumstances, individuals of black appearance were indeed over represented in the police figures when compared to white and other visible minority groups. However, what was not measured was the street population in terms of numbers of white and minority ethnic individuals who were actually using the streets at the time the stops were made. If the police genuinely believe that the stop and search tactic is a worthwhile detection and prevention tactic in areas where streets are regularly used by suspects, then it is inevitable that the largest proportion of those stopped will be from the ethnic group who represent the majority of people using the streets at the relevant times. If the police are indeed racist, as many of their critics would claim, then it is likely that the converse would be apparent. On streets where non-black people predominate, if indeed the police are being racially discriminatory, then it would be expected that a disproportionate number of individuals from visible minority ethnic groups would be stopped and searched. In other words, individuals from minority ethnic groups are being selected for stop and search in preference to the majority of street users.

The issue of stop and search is obviously very important for the police and public. Therefore, it is equally important to ensure the statistics that describe and elaborate the picture conform to the best practices of that discipline. It is a matter for the police to ensure that their activities are properly measured and that the conclusions drawn from the data are accurately presented. If the police produce a written press release quoting statistics in support of a particular situation, it must be sufficiently detailed to enable users to properly understand both the issue and the context in which the events took place. Leaving out detail in the belief that it will confuse or obscure a message is tempting observers to make judgments that reinforce their own pre-conceived ideas, rather than reporting the facts. A worse situation, however, is created when government publish statistics on behalf of the police that are incomplete, misleading, at too high a level of abstraction, or lacking context. In such situations, police attempts to counteract misleading reports appear excessively defensive and un-professional.

A further data difficulty can arise in similar circumstances that can present a problem for the police and other criminal justice organisations to counteract without appearing confrontational or defensive. For instance, the rate at which cases are discontinued at magistrates and crown courts is an important statistic. This type of outcome can arise for a number of reasons, some unavoidable and outside the control of any participating agency, others may arise from carelessness or incomplete prosecution evidence. So, the Crown Prosecution Service (CPS) are interested to know when the discontinuance rate is rising or falling, as clearly a falling, or static low rate, would be desirable from their point of view, which would tend to indicate that their prosecution decisions are sound. Conversely, the police will consider a case to be cleared up when a person is charged or summoned to court, regardless of the outcome of the prosecution (providing certain conditions are met within the Home Office counting rules), and clearly an increasing clear-up rate is preferable for the police. However, it is in the interest of the CPS to show that an increasing discontinuance rate is not their responsibility, but rather that of the police due to some flaw in investigations. The police then argue that the decision to prosecute in the first place is that of the CPS and it is not their responsibility if, say, court adjournments cause problems for witnesses, or it is decided not to prosecute for some other reason. Such disagreements are hopefully isolated, but it does show how the selection of performance indicators needs to be made with some care and diligence and that the statistic is actually measuring an occurrence that is insightful and not something that is being skewed by influences outside of control. In short, care must be taken to ensure that when something that makes one organisation look efficient, it is not giving the opposite impression regarding another when this is not an accurate assessment

It is probably true to say that statistics generally, and detailed statistics in particular, are not always the easiest medium to convey with both interest and precision. Indeed, for some, the very mention of a statistic provokes immediate disinterest, or even spontaneous cynicism, arising from the belief that most, if not all, official statistics are biased in favour of government. It is therefore asking a great deal of the police to rise above this background, but they must do so if an accurate representation is to be made of their efforts.

As has been noted, capturing statistics relevant to the quantity of demands falling on police, such as the incidence of crimes, traffic collisions, assaults, and disorder, etc. is generally not difficult, but neither is this data useful for management purposes at a high level of aggregation. Caution is also necessary if computer assisted recording procedures are used, which can facilitate some very fast, voluminous, but equally useless analysis. However, what is much more difficult to measure is the *quality* of the service that has been provided. Here again, governments in the past have been guilty of making some misleading assumptions about police activity based on a flawed belief about the value of what police actually do. For instance, during the last decade, it was assumed that those police forces who had the highest clear up rates for recorded crime were the most effective. Amongst other things, this statistic completely ignores the impact that these relative degrees of police success have on victims and thus the value to society. It is not possible to make the assumption from this measure that a police force that solves proportionately more crime than another is more effective. For instance, in an area where there is a high incidence of recorded street robberies, including snatching of personal bags, police may have to direct considerable resources to surveillance and observation before suspects might be identified. In another area, there might be, say, a high incidence of retail theft, or similar personal thefts in retail complexes, which, given the preponderance of CCTV in many shops, might make detection a much more straightforward process. However, to aggregate this data and then to compare them is really very misleading, and yet such practices have been very common at government level and not effectively challenged by the police.

A partial solution to such difficulties is provided by the Home Office's 'National Crime Survey', which simplistically may be described as a victim survey. Amongst other things, a representative sample of the population are invited to participate in a questionnaire-driven survey, which seeks to answer such questions as the rate of un-reported crime and victim attitudes to crime and police responses. Again, the problem here is the very high level of aggregation used in the presentation of the results that sometimes produce startling headlines, but very little in the way of new information that the police might action. One of the few useful features useful of this device are in those aspects of the survey that are consistently statistically reliable, in that the results are comparable over time, thus showing growing or diminishing trends.

Having been somewhat critical of attempts at measurement of policing activity and performance, it is perhaps appropriate to offer some suggestions as to how this situation might be improved. Clearly measuring everything that happens to, or within, a police organisation is not a realistic prospect, and even if it were, it would be extremely difficult to analyse and assimilate the conclusions. Measurement, therefore, should be confined to those demands, activities, and outcomes that are critical to the understanding of organisational effectiveness. In Chapter One, a plea was made for more easily digestible strategy documents to be produced by police forces which contain a limited number of achievable priorities that could be readily understood by police and public alike. In the event that such refinement was achieved, measurement of demands and performance becomes a much more straightforward matter. When setting priorities, it becomes important to specify what data will be used to assess success and how the analysis will be undertaken. By this means, it is possible to reduce the amount of effort that is put into data collection and data storage; it also prevents that other great statistical temptation, that of embarking on data 'fishing trips', which, of course, are so much more easily achieved through computers with powerful analytical software. It is clearly desirable to have as few people as possible engaged on measuring things and as many as possible focused on priorities, so the careful selection of what actually is measured is important.

There are two statistical methods that will assist considerably with the production of cost effective management data and which will prompt relevant questions through the analysis; those of sampling and trend forecasting. Sampling techniques have not been widely used in police organisations, aside from some survey research; it is not clear whether this is due to a reticence to trust sample data, or whether it is just the ease with which large volumes of data can be electronically stored. As has been noted, however, it simply does not make any sense to store vast volumes of data in the belief that some of it might come in useful one day, or that it has been useful in the past. Large quantities of data can be difficult to analyse and confusing to understand. It would be so much more efficient to draw sample data from whatever source is necessary, according to the priorities that have been set for the organisation. Such sample data, if repeated reliably, might then be set in a time series to provide an opportunity for forecasting. A valuable management tool is thus created whereby trends might be identified. As mentioned previously, it might be observed whether an increased deployment of police to a particular location at particular times achieved a measurable change in whatever problem was being experienced. Conversely, if the withdrawal of routine police activity from defined locations or problems resulted in a negligible alteration to demands on police, a judgment might then be made as to the value of those particular deployments. In a similar vein, if time series are used to make forecasts about rising or falling trends, deployments can be adjusted to either prevent predicted increases, or to withdraw from unproductive activities. Similarly, redeployments might be made when identified problems have abated, or shown a reducing trend. Such management methods are straightforward, but they are a break away from the administratively convenient, traditional methods of police patrol deployment and the large element of discretionary patrol activity that currently takes place. During earlier generations of policing it was doubtless possible for local officers to use their extensive local knowledge to make such decisions without the benefit of data. However, the breadth and complexity of policing demands today, coupled with the transfer of police between different functions and locations, means that data must provide the knowledge that was previously held at local police stations by locally, long serving police officers. Many commercial companies rely on the routine use of data to make key decisions about their activities. Commercial airlines, for instance, rely on weather forecasts and historic air traffic volumes to make decisions about aircraft fuel loads; clearly a significant factor to both profitability and safety. Given that such a critical issue for aviation is data driven, it seems far less risky for police to utilise a similar approach.

As has been explained, demand, deployment, and activity measurement is, of course, essential to the management of an efficient and effective police organisation. As described in Chapter One, however, if it is accepted that the unique and fundamental characteristic of UK policing is that of '*policing by consent*', then it is equally essential to determine, by both qualitative and quantitative means, whether this is in fact happening and whether or not there are any positive or negative trends emerging in this respect. The only really cost effective means of answering these questions is by survey methods, applied to respondents who have been victims, or others who come into contact with the police, together with a local control sample, who have not had any meaningful contact with the police. Carefully constructed questionnaires, administered by professional research organisations, would be able to provide reliable time series information that could address all these points in a cost effective manner. The amount of public money that would need to be expended on obtaining such information, which would lead to more efficient and effective policing, is trivial when compared with the cost of 'trial and error policing', or worse still, making costly assumptions that are convenient to the police for whatever reason.

Comparatively small samples of survey data, accumulated

regularly, could provide valuable information regarding police activity and strategy. It is important to point out here that this is not suggested as a public relations exercise, although such methods might have a positive effect in this respect; it is intended as a management tool to assist in gaining the best outcomes with scarce resources. The emphasis to achieve this therefore has to be upon local communities. As established previously, over-aggregated activity data is practically useless for decision making purposes and the same is true for survey research data. The information obtained from such surveys has to be sufficiently precise in terms of location in order that residents' responses might be separated from visitors' responses and each can in turn can be sub-divided into the various categories of individuals who have, or who have not, recently experienced contact with the police.

The opportunities presented by the widespread use of the internet, mobile phones, especially 'smart' phones, and other mobile devices present a range of opportunities for such data to be gathered easily on a regular basis. Such applications might be extended to the creation of 'expert panels' that might be established to provide the police with feedback on particular topics. Here again, provided the sample base is constructed using statistically sound methods, the results could be valuable for decision making and the development of fresh strategies.

There is really nothing for the police to lose by exploring and developing such methods to enhance their service delivery and measure their effectiveness. The only danger is in not asking the questions and making assumptions about what the public want and how they want the service delivered.

8.

Technologies and Procurement

How to Tool Up

It is unavoidable that any major organisation can ignore the advantages that might accrue by exploiting technologies relevant to their operation and policing is no exception. In the respect of policing and police organisations, the term technology is taken to have a conventional definition, in that it is the application of science that is relevant to police activities, including the operation of police organisations themselves. Police organisations are generally not, however, developers, producers, or suppliers of technological equipment. Meaning that, as many others, they have to purchase or acquire what they need from businesses in the private technology sector. Therefore, the process of identifying which particular problem is amenable to a technological solution, what is essential or desirable, who produces it, how much it costs, and how it will be procured is a significant issue for police efficiency and effectiveness. This chapter explores some of the issues behind these questions and offers some proposals as to how current arrangements might be improved.

It is tempting to think of technology, as applied to policing, as those forensic tools used by investigators for crime detection purposes, such as the national DNA database. The scope of police-related technologies is, however, much wider. For instance, the application and analysis of CCTV material, identification applications, such as facial and vehicle number recognition systems, automated fingerprint retrieval systems, less than lethal devices (such as TASARs), radio and data transmission systems, together with the conventional infrastructure data systems that would be found in any large, modern organisation. Typically finance, payroll, human resources, fleet management, stock control, internet access, office systems, document production, and so forth. Such computer-based applications are able to significantly add to the efficiency of a police organisation and their acquisition and use is hardly a choice, as without the speed and accuracy of data retrieval from such systems, modern police forces would be unable to function. The discussion here will therefore be confined to those existing and potential applications, where choices do have to be made and where equipment development is not complete.

There is a department of the Home Office that is responsible, in their own words, "...for keeping the police and their other customers at least one step ahead of the criminal..." This objective is regrettably far from realisation. Generally speaking, each UK police force is responsible for identifying its own technology requirements and procuring the necessary equipment from the private sector. There are a few notable exceptions to this approach in which the Home Office has been deeply involved in order to achieve a single, national standard. Examples include the national police radio system 'Airwave', the personal CS spray issued to all police officers, and the less than lethal device commonly known as 'Taser'. Other examples that concern internal data storage and retrieval systems, which necessitate national data and storage standards, including the national DNA database, the national automated fingerprint system, and of course the national criminal record system, which is maintained by a Home Office agency. However, surprising as it may seem, there are multiple versions of police systems, produced by different suppliers, and purchased by different police forces, according to what they perceive as their peculiar local need. This accumulation of different systems has had the effect, over several decades, of creating an incompatible patchwork of police data applications around the country where interoperability is difficult, if not impossible to achieve. Police in Scotland have experienced this frustration consequent upon the amalgamation of the former eight separate regional police forces into a single organisation.

Recent attempts to achieve a national police intelligence database have also run into difficulties, largely because individual police forces store and analyse intelligence information on different producers' software. It is quite surprising that if police intelligence staff in one part of the UK are asked to produce a specification for an intelligence database system, it is likely to be markedly different to the same requirement, but produced by a different police force, in another part of the country. This is especially surprising in respect of intelligence, as there is a national standard for storing and categorising intelligence information. In fact, there are examples of police forces actually refusing to accept computerised applications that have been developed for others on the basis of not much more than it was 'not invented here', or that it 'doesn't meet our local need'. These issues, and others, have played a major part in constraining the development of national systems that are fully inter-operative. Some may argue that it is a positive aspect of policing in the UK that many data systems are not interoperable, as this contributes to the protection of individual freedoms and constrains police operations from becoming too ambitious. However, in business terms and in providing value for money for the taxpayer, it is far from efficient.

A common problem that has accounted for much delay, frustration, and unnecessary cost in the development of common police data systems, is that of the police over specifying their need, or in the worst examples, altering the requirement during development. Insistence on particular features, which would only be relevant to a limited number of users and which, in reality, would seldom be of significance, have accounted for an embarrassingly large number of delays and even cancellations of national applications.

On one hand, therefore, it seems individual police forces have a very clear idea of what they need by way of data systems and other technologies, yet most police officers and staff have little idea of what the information, communications, and security suppliers can provide by way of new developments. It seems, therefore, that the police as a whole are locked into a stagnant situation that is unlikely to alter without radical change to development and procurement methods.

Some of the police operational difficulties associated with computer and communications based technologies are discussed in chapters Five and Six, but a significant issue to note here is that many criminals who are technologically literate have taken advantage of the police's failure to have pro-active technology strategies. Typically, the growth in the commission of computer/internet based fraud may be seen not only as a function of the rapid expansion of computer and communications technologies, but of also the failure of the police in particular to stay '...one step ahead of the criminal...'.

A significant issue is therefore to ask how do the police know what they need and how do they find out about where and how to procure it? The answer in part is that there is an element of the police invariably having to catch up with technology. For example, if a fraud is perpetrated using the facility of, say, a smart phone, then the police will respond by ensuring they have the facilities to analyse data held on the device, so in future they will be better equipped to tackle that type of crime. If, however, fraud is not a particular priority for a provincial police force, then it is unlikely that this type of technology will be widely accessible and thus available for use in investigating other types of crime. It is frequently the case that the major driver for technology acquisition is the recent experience of officers involved in a particularly challenging investigation. In such cases, officers have to use their own initiative and creativity to find solutions to operational problems that have not been previously encountered, and if the solution is some form of computer application, then the motivation to specify a complete user requirement increases. A good example here is the time consuming activity of reviewing CCTV footage product, which led to the creation of software packages that have the capability to search such data for specific details, allowing officers to concentrate on the relevant sections. This does, of course, present further challenges in respect of disclosure (Chapter Six), but did produce an efficient solution to a particularly laborious task. However, the officers and police staff involved in the high volume of such work are generally the more junior in rank and therefore not involved in procurement of equipment, or even influential in the decisions of what is purchased and what is not. The outcome regrettably is that the police are destined to always be behind the criminal in technology acquisition if this situation persists.

Businesses in the so-called 'hi tech' sector customarily display their capabilities at police and security exhibitions and advertise in the various journals that specialise in supporting their work. Generally speaking, these events and advertising sources are only visited or seen by police officers and staff who are themselves specialists in technology functions. This means that the operational staff, who are the people actually tackling the day-to-day problems, are not the individuals who are exposed to the potential solutions or capabilities. In effect, problems and potential corresponding solutions are frequently not recognised for each other anything like quickly enough.

This difficulty presents frustrating challenges for business as well as police organisations. Businesses frequently have solutions for problems that the police are experiencing but do not have any means of bringing the solution to the attention of anyone inside the police who might influence or decide upon procurement. As previously discussed, the problem to be solved is probably in the hands of an operational person, who will be difficult to contact by a sales or marketing person from industry. Even if contact is made, the chances are that there will not be the opportunity to fully explain the potential benefits of the proposed solution, much less the opportunity for any sort of demonstration of capabilities. Indeed, operational staff would be extremely guarded about discussing this type of issue with an unknown person who has made a 'cold call'. Even if it transpires that a particular product does indeed meet an operational requirement, there are myriad stages of formal procurement processes to be applied before the product is available for operational use. Indeed, it is quite clear that many businesses simply do not understand the constraints that apply to police procurement procedures and the authority levels that have to be negotiated. It is likely that this particular problem arises because police staff involved with procurement are not sufficiently open with suppliers about their procedures and use the bureaucracy as a means of defence from potentially 'pushy' suppliers. In a similar vein, it might be questioned how much attention commercial organisations give to understanding how police procurement systems operate. Whatever the cause, the consequence is that so often, by the time the solution has been implemented, it is quite likely that the nature of the original operational problem will have altered and those involved moved on to other pressing issues, or other aspects of criminality. In much the same way as career criminals migrate from committing one type of crime to another depending on their perceived risk of detection. For instance, fraud is now perceived as less risky to commit than, say, cash in transit and bank robberies with potentially greater proceeds.

Failure to react, or reacting too slowly to technological innovation, has hampered operational policing in many ways. Limited and incompatible intelligence systems, computer and portable electronic device analysis, and CCTV data analysis are just a few examples of where the police have not been aware of industrial capabilities and have had to struggle to slowly realise the benefits. Much less to take advantage of rapid results fed back to detectives to hasten the development of their investigations.

It is generally accepted by many businesses in the technology sector that selling to police organisations is often a frustrating and fruitless experience. Generally, police officers and staff do not warm to sales people, who are seen to promise everything and then only deliver partial solutions. There is also a common feeling amongst many police people associated with technological applications that businesses in this sector are adept at re-packaging solutions designed for other clients and then selling the package to the police as a bespoke application; over promising and under delivering. Conversely, technology sales and marketing people frequently see police staff as suspicious, guarded, overly bureaucratic, and capable of being unpredictable.

There are, of course, exceptions, and where productive partnerships have been formed, some quite innovative solutions to complex problems have evolved. For instance, the display of the 'Crimestoppers' logo on commercial and personal desktop computers, and perhaps in the future, on mobile devices, so criminality and suspicions can be quickly and anonymously reported. Regrettably, however, there are as many examples where innovative solutions have not been implemented. In some instances, there has been severe public criticism of some senior officers who have tried to champion one technological solution over another, resulting in an almost paranoid reluctance amongst senior police and police staff not to involve themselves in any sort of dialogue with business in the fear they will be accused of seeking some sort of personal advantage. Whether this is accepting hospitality, seeking employment after retirement from the police, gaining an unfair advantage for a friend or relative; the list of fears is lengthy. The outcome is, of course, that little that is innovative or pro-active is apparent. There is an institutionalised avoidance of failure, so the practice of piloting technological solutions in police organisations is rare. The prospect of being criticised for spending money on a trial system that later fails is an outcome most people in police organisations would actively avoid, despite the knowledge and advantage that might accrue from such tests. Given this bleak analysis, it is hardly surprising the police lag behind in exploiting technologies for operational benefit.

It is clear that the police are not the only public sector group that suffers from this technology malaise. Much attention has been given to the apparent failure or late delivery of a number of large scale computer systems procured by government departments, including the police. Doubtless, there are many reasons why these failures have been experienced and probably as many reports claiming, with the benefit of hindsight, what went wrong. On one hand, suppliers asserting that the requirement kept changing and, on the other, clients complaining that costs continued to rise beyond estimates. Both sides admitting, for their own reasons, that time-scales slipped, creating further costs. The outcome being that inefficiencies continue when solutions are available.

Regardless of the reasons, the fact remains that the police generally are not efficient at procuring technology solutions to both operational and support service functions. The former Association of Chief Police Officers (ACPO) to some extent recognised this difficulty and appointed a small number of their members to take the lead nationally on particular topics that have likely technological solutions or implications. The problem here returns to the characteristic of local police parochialism. The lead officers for particular topics are likely to establish small committees of specialists to advise them, but of course not everyone can be represented. The likely outcome being a response from at least some police forces '…that it is not like that here…', or '…we have other priorities…'. It is also a feature of this arrangement that the lead officer can seldom give full attention to the issues arising and must rely on others to become involved in discovering opportunities and solutions. The chief officers will all have full time appointments within their own police forces and they will have to create time in their own busy work schedules to address these potentially complicated issues on behalf of the police service as a whole. In short, it is simply not that easy to achieve agreement on technological solutions that have national application, which is why the Home Office has taken up the task of specifying and procuring major systems on behalf of the police in the past. A possible faster model may lie in the specification and procurement of back-office functions on a regional basis.

It is reasonable to consider that, for some national police computer based applications, a bespoke system would have to be designed, tested, and then implemented, necessitating the creation of a detailed user requirement. This process in itself may take many months, if not years, to produce, research, negotiate, agree, and finalise. However, if police solutions and applications are to follow the trend of both private sector companies and the technology sector itself, the concept of bespoke solutions will not be a feature of the future.

It seems that very few of the applications that many people and businesses regularly use, either on their desktop computers or their portable devices, have been designed as bespoke solutions to identified problems. Rather, development has been undertaken by the computer industry on the basis of its own creativity, and the products launched to succeed or fail on their merits and utility. Thereby the industry accepts the risk and is rewarded by the profit if the product succeeds and a market is created. If successful, this occurs regardless of whether the final users of the product had identified a need for it prior to having the opportunity to use it. Such an approach doubtless has the potential to meet the needs of police solutions, but the problem is in providing access to police operations and activities in order for the industry to better understand the issues and complexities of the problems and indeed where creative applications might put police ahead of the criminals. It seems this is not an insoluble problem. It must be possible to devise a vetting and licensing system for businesses to be allowed to gain access to police organisations in order to assess how technology might improve efficiency and effectiveness. Indeed, there is already in existence a mandatory vetting system for government suppliers of information technology and other systems that concern classified data. This vetting system, like many others, is a mystery to many business people and those outside government departments. There is no doubting the importance of protecting police systems from rogue and counterfeit software, but vetting and security awareness may overcome this risk to a large extent. The vetting process is doubtless a barrier to some of the smaller technology suppliers from gaining opportunities for business from government departments, including the police. It is, of course, so often the case that it is the smaller suppliers who are the innovators, but who cannot, for a barrier of bureaucratic reasons, gain access to government markets and opportunities. The bureaucrats would doubtless argue that it is only the largest suppliers that have the resilience and the experience to work on official applications, when what they really mean is that the large prime contractors represent the safest choice for the Civil Service.

The police desperately need access to progressive and innovative technological solutions and this might be achieved at very low cost to the taxpayer by opening police organisations to the scrutiny of those in a position to assist. Issues regarding vetting, intellectual property rights, pilot trials, contracts, licenses, and future sales are all soluble if the will is present to exploit the skills of the technology sector. It is simply not efficient for the police to hang onto traditional methods of specification and procurement that lag so far behind operational needs. The UK military have procedures for meeting urgent operational requirements, and there is no justifiable reason for the police not having the same ability. This particular point perhaps arises from the fact that there are senior military officers and staff advising ministers in the Ministry of Defence, but there are not any senior police officers performing a similar role within the Home Office. It might be argued that the Home Office could consult the National Police Chiefs Council (NPCC) subject lead officers, if it were minded to do so, and no doubt this happens from time to time, but of course this will only be in response to questions, rather than providing an opportunity for original or creative exchanges between police, ministers, and civil servants. Although only of historic interest, this situation was characterised by the failure of the Home Office to procure an automated fingerprint retrieval system during the 1990s. The consequence was that a number of individual forces formed a consortium to draw on a facility in the USA, where such systems had been in use for some time. Clearly a desperate solution to improve crime clear-ups in the face of an obstinate Home Office.

An obvious example of where such collaboration might be enormously beneficial is in the exploitation of CCTV technologies for crime prevention purposes. The industry that supports CCTV technologies have created a range of innovative applications that, given the active co-operation of the police and the support of government, might make a significant impact on the incidence of some crimes and the detection and conviction of offenders. Such schemes as 'trap houses' and 'trap vehicles', deploying concealed cameras to identify offenders, have proved successful. Miniaturised, concealed cameras incorporated into bank ATMs provide a straightforward means of yielding evidence in relation to bank card frauds and, of course, the associated crimes concerning bag and wallet snatches in order to obtain the cards. There are many other straightforward applications, such as automatic vehicle number plate recognition systems (ANPR), that given the willingness of government, the police and the CCTV industry might provide improved reassurance to the public, as well as having a direct impact on crime and crime prevention. As mentioned earlier, such initiatives as the wider use of 'Crimestoppers' could speed up and enhance reports of suspects and suspicions. 'Crimestoppers' is a well-established charity that understands police operations by exploiting technological opportunities and could significant further contribute to police effectiveness. However, such methods are not without complication. The laws concerning public privacy, data protection, and the guidance from the Information Commissioner's Office are far from clear, with a good deal of such evidence obtained by CCTV being challenged in courts on the basis of breaches of these provisions and the associated codes of practice. It seems, therefore, that the only way that crime prevention measures might be enhanced through exploiting these technologies is with the co-operation of government. and its ability to harmonise the policies of the various Whitehall departments concerned. Clearly, neither the police nor the CCTV industry has the ability to create any form of scheme, and to establish best practice, without government support. Similarly, the capability of computerised major crime investigation systems to firewall an application for defence evidence disclosure purposes would doubtless be of significant benefit, but such a solution requires the active involvement across diverse government departments. This regrettable state of affairs doubtless explains why, so far, only relatively small-scale pilot schemes exploiting these technologies have been implemented. They are cost effective, efficient, and have proven benefit to public safety; all that is lacking is the government will to grasp some of the difficulties.

9.

Rights and Wrongs

Who polices the police?

It is clearly necessary, in any democratic and tolerant society, that those responsible for enforcing the established law do so lawfully themselves. When this is not evident, it is equally important that there are systems in place that facilitate the investigation of any alleged negligence or wrongdoing. Such systems must be formalised and be easily accessible to people who feel they have a grievance against the police, whether the accusations are justified or not. Such a facility is in contrast to the circumstances in many other countries, where the police themselves are the arbiters of what is tolerable and what is not and complaints against them are considered trivial and just ignored. It is easy to imagine how frustrating it would be to have a legitimate grievance against the police for being, say, unnecessarily heavy handed or overbearing and without access to a channel of redress, or no means of expressing the complaint to a responsible authority. So, an independent police complaints system is a fundamentally important feature that supports the philosophy of policing by consent. If, on one hand, the police are able to pursue their responsibilities with the passive consent of the public, then there must be a counter balancing system for the public to have redress when police act in a way that is without such consent; unlawfully, wrongly, or overbearingly. The principal of an independent police complaints system is therefore reasonably straightforward to establish, but the practicalities of realising an efficient and effective system are somewhat more vexed.

During the past few decades, there has been a steady stream of changes to the procedures for addressing police wrongdoing. Certainly during the working life of many currently serving police officers, the system for investigating complaints from the public about police misconduct has changed significantly. Historically, individual police forces were almost entirely responsible for investigating complaints made against their own police officers, with the most serious allegations being referred to another force for investigation. Where criminal allegations were involved, the investigation file would be referred to the Director of Public Prosecutions (DPP) for a decision as to further investigation or prosecution. A series of alterations to this system has now led to a completely independent investigation organisation, the Independent Police Complaints Commission. (IPCC) that was re-titled in 2017 to 'The Independent Office for Police Conduct (IOPC)'. This body is responsible for handling their own investigations into serious and potentially criminal complaints against police and for overseeing less serious complaints that continue to be investigated by dedicated professional standards departments within individual police forces. Typically, a police professional standards department would report to the deputy chief constable of a police force, who would be independently responsible for decision making in relation to complaints and discipline issues. This arrangement leaves the chief constable unsighted on the detail of an investigation and therefore able to chair any disciplinary hearing, or appeal, that might follow. Although this does not preclude the IOPC from directing that a chief constable from another force should preside or, more usually, that an independent person should chair proceedings with an independent panel appointed.

These changes to the police complaints system have undoubtedly led to a far greater degree of thoroughness in the investigation of alleged misconduct and brought about an independence from the police themselves to the process of complaint enquiry. Public confidence in the system has doubtless increased and, generally speaking, the police themselves have welcomed the presentational improvements that at least have dispelled the suggestion that the police are responsible for policing themselves.

However, the current system is not without its difficulties for both police and public.

From a police perspective, the IOPC can be seen as a fairly limited organisation, both in terms of capacity, ability, and professionalism. Many of the investigators, who have significant legal powers to pursue their enquiries, are retired police officers themselves and not always seen as the most diligent. Those who are not former police officers can be seen as lacking investigative skills and often misled by carefully constructed, but mischievous or vexatious allegations. Such complaints frequently arise from complainants and witnesses, who either simply want to cause trouble for the police or, more deviously, to use the complaints system as an element in their own defence of a criminal allegation. Probably the principal difficulty experienced by the accused police officer(s) is the protracted nature of many of the IOPC procedures, frequently leaving officers wondering what is happening for months or, exceptionally, even years. Generally, complaint investigations that are not of a criminal nature, but concern procedural or discipline matters, are not progressed until after any criminal investigation and proceedings against the complainant have been concluded, thus potentially extending the period of uncertainty even longer. Needless to say, the effect on morale and productivity is significant and often extends to colleagues that are not the subject of the complaint themselves, but who are associated with the accused officer(s). Whether these frequent and long delays are the result of resource constraints, or just a dilatory culture at the IOPC, is not clear, but in any event, the affect is similar. It seems that the reluctance to treat officers in a courteous way lies at the heart of much of the police dissatisfaction with the practicalities of the system. Few police officers and staff would deny the appropriateness of an independent oversight of complaints, or an independent investigation of more serious matters, but not being informed as to progress is a common frustration. Similarly, the seizure of personal possessions, such as passports, smart phones, and computers, which prove to be of no evidential value and which are not returned for protracted periods, is a cause of much anxiety. Again, the lack of opportunity to find out exactly what is happening adds to the feeling of uncertainty, especially if the officer or staff member is suspended from duty while the investigation is progressed.

These issues lead to the supposition that many investigations conducted by the IOPC, and its precursor organisation, are not adequately supervised. The so-called 'commissioners' of the IOPC are responsible for oversight of investigations, but many are comparatively inexperienced in conducting investigations themselves and it is therefore difficult to appreciate how they can provide the necessary oversight, support, and leadership that would characterise a police-supervised investigation. Conventionally, a major police investigation would be subject to terms of reference that would be reviewed on a regular basis by the senior investigating officer. Such terms of reference are designed to keep an investigation on course and to avoid losing focus on the main lines of enquiry. This straightforward discipline does not seem to be a feature of IOPC investigations, which often appear to wander away from the main allegations. This style of investigation, which includes exploration for prejudicial information against the accused officer, can be very damaging, as it often appears that the investigators are searching for anything that might be used in a negative way against the police suspect. Of course, investigations must be rigorous, but such practices would not be tolerated in a conventional criminal investigation and many officers find it difficult to understand why they should be subject to such tactics. Indeed, criminal allegations against officers have been dismissed at crown court where the officers' defence has successfully argued that the weight of prejudicial information against the accused has been dis-proportionate, yet the practice seems to continue un-checked

The problem of overzealous investigations into police misconduct has become more apparent during the past few years, with the IOPC using their powers of arrest in what appears to be an unnecessary and inexperienced way. As mentioned earlier, because a legal power exists, it doesn't mean it has to be used. Arrest, for instance, is frequently used to ensure a suspect is made amenable to justice and to provide a power to search. However, the reputational and psychological damage experienced after such a tactic is used against a police employee has to be weighed against the alternative methods available, the likelihood of a loss of evidence, and the probability of a repeat offence. This is not to say that police officers suspected of criminality should be treated differently from other members of the public in similar circumstances, but it must be recalled that one of principal characteristics of a police person is that of personal integrity. If such a value is brought into question by arrest, the reputation of that individual will be lastingly damaged, even if innocent, making the resumption of a police career extremely difficult. The arrest of police officers for criminal offences, such as misconduct in a public office, is an example of such heavy handedness. The CPS and the Court of Appeal have both made it quite clear that the use of this offence should be '...strictly confined...' and that the seriousness of the alleged acts or omissions should be carefully considered. The implication being that the bar is set very high for this particular offence to be satisfied and therefore also the corresponding power of arrest that is attached to the offence.

Such examples of over zealousness regrettably do not enhance the reputation of the IOPC in the eyes of the police; experienced police investigators would generally not tolerate such overbearing use of powers. Of more concern to police officers is that it is not clear how an officer who is dis-satisfied with an IOPC investigation might bring concerns to notice, either during the course of an investigation or indeed afterwards. As a partial remedy, the police staff associations are usually able to provide legal advice through retained lawyers and conventionally an officer will be allocated a liaison contact in more serious allegations. However, feelings of isolation, helplessness, and unfairness, accompanied by depression, are common anxieties expressed by police officers and police staff who are accused of wrongdoing. Extremely severe manifestations of these conditions have resulted in credible suicide attempts. A most unpleasant situation is created by the inappropriate use of such tactics if an officer is arrested at his or her home by the IOPC. In such circumstances, the suspect officer would be taken to their local police custody centre for documentation and questioning. This, of course, immediately reveals the IOPC suspicions to the local police and the reputation of a local resident officer is consequently damaged. The local police will not have access to the investigations progress, or whether the officer is subsequently cleared of the criminal allegations, leaving a lingering question mark over the arrested officer. As previously noted, in an occupation where personal integrity is paramount, such treatment of an innocent individual can be ruinous to both personal and professional life.

It is not only the police, however, who find the systems for complaint investigation less than satisfactory. Frequently, members of the public who come into contact with the police and who are, for one reason or another, dis-satisfied with the service or treatment they receive, find it difficult to understand the complaint investigation procedure, despite the explanatory leaflets. There is an apparently easily available means by which such people can bring their complaint to attention, either personally by telephone, or by letter or e-mail. All such complaints are recorded and all are subject to scrutiny by the professional standards department of the relevant police force. Depending on the nature of the allegation, a decision is made as to whether the matter will be referred to the IOPC or dealt with locally. In some cases, the IOPC may direct that another police force should investigate, or they may decide to oversee an investigation by the local force concerned. In any event, the matter should not be ignored, so at least there is an opportunity for reliable scrutiny of the circumstances of any complaint.

Most regrettably, however, it is becoming more frequent for some types of criminal behaviour or misconduct by police to be brushed aside, either by the officer initially receiving the complaint, or the internal professional standards departments. It has been widely reported that incidents of flirtatious behaviour towards female victims and vulnerable females, improper suggestions of a sexual nature, and in some circumstances, incidents of indecent exposure and even assault are being ignored by an institutionally misogynistic culture across the whole of policing. This is clearly a very broad and serious criticism and may be an exaggeration, but that does not in any way dilute the seriousness of any such allegation or the importance of thoroughly investigating every one, regardless of the origins or context of the allegation. For instance, it might be tempting to consider behaviour at a social event, or inappropriate language at a sporting event, to be of less significance and therefore excusable. This is, however, definitely incorrect. It is simply not possible for a police officer to alter their views when on duty and to harbour unacceptable views in their private life. An officer who shouts racist abuse at a televised football match when alone is just as culpable and unwelcome in the police as someone behaving in that way at a public stadium.

The police are subject to a discipline, or professional standards code, that essentially specifies how police officers should conduct themselves and set about their work. The code covers matters that do not necessarily amount to criminal offences, but actions and behaviours that are not desirable conduct for police. Rudeness or inappropriate language, overbearing conduct, neglect of duty, bringing the police into disrepute, failing to carry out a lawful order, and various rules regarding appearance and sobriety are all matters covered by the professional standards policy. Usually when an officer is subject to a complaint that concerns a disciplinary matter, the investigation will be carried out locally and any subsequent finding of guilt by an internal disciplinary board will be communicated to the complainant, whether public or police. In more serious matters, the IOPC may direct that the disciplinary hearing is open to the public. In which case, the complainant may well understand more of the process than might otherwise be the case. However, it is commonly suggested by police that the presiding chair of such disciplinary tribunals is likely to be more lenient than a chief constable. In effect, this means that the benefits of openness and transparency are offset by an insufficiently robust message to the wider police community about the behaviours that will not be tolerated.

It seems that the major problem experienced by the public, when complaints are made about the police, is similar to the concerns of the police themselves, in that they seldom know what is happening. As already mentioned, some of the investigations and decision making processes can be very protracted and complainants are frequently left wondering whether the matter is actually being progressed, or whether it is no longer important. Clearly, some professional standards departments will try to avoid this irritation by keeping complainants in touch with progress, but more often than not, the public will express exasperation with what seems a dilatory procedure. In the interim, of course, their dissatisfaction with the police often manifests as a lack of support for the police generally, open criticism, and an understandable reluctance to become involved in anything to do with the police, possibly to the detriment of other victims' cases where perhaps they might help as witnesses.

It is often said by police officers that, on occasions, the only advantage an investigator has is confidentiality, in that the suspect or accused person does not know where, or in which direction the investigation is progressing. Such parochial wisdom does, however, interfere with the public's general need to know what is happening when they have complained about the police. It seems that there is a culture in both professional standards departments and the IOPC to be as secretive as possible and a consequence of this is that complainants become dissatisfied with the process.

Much might be done to avoid such accusations and to reveal more of the complaints system to the public. For instance, a very swift response to complainants' concerns may often result in an official complaint being withdrawn, especially if it concerns a minor matter. If a complaint is received and an immediate 'scoping investigation' is undertaken to establish whether the accusations are accurate, it may be that the officer complained about has acted in good faith and that the complainant has not fully understood the procedure that the officer followed. Complainants are often unfamiliar with and confused by police procedures, which might not have been adequately explained. In which case, it is possible to mistake the officers' behaviour as inappropriate in some way. For instance, if a member of the public makes an emergency call for police, but there is a significant delay in response, it may be that the complainant will see this as the fault of the officer(s) who did eventually arrive. A quick examination of the radio logs around the time in question might reveal that every operational asset was indeed fully occupied on other pressing matters and that the response was made as quickly as possible. A prompt explanation to such a complainant will often be sufficient, leaving both sides satisfied with the outcome, which was not perhaps ideal but nevertheless understandable. In fact, many well managed professional standards departments will operate such practices and all such matters will be recorded and subject to scrutiny by the deputy chief constable, and through the offices of the Police and Crime Commissioner, as a check on whether more serious matters are being inappropriately handled in this way. Clearly, if the allegation is substantial, such an approach will also have benefits in that potential loss of evidence might be avoided, in much the same way as for a conventional criminal investigation. The underlying principal should be one of responding promptly and quickly testing the allegation.

More difficult to handle, though, are allegations made by defendants or witnesses in court proceedings. It is not uncommon for defendants to manufacture all sorts of false accounts of police behaviour as a means of discrediting police witnesses and weakening the prosecution case. Allegations of assault, organising conspiracies to the detriment of the accused, accepting inducements, and planting evidence, typically drugs or knives, are all a part of the experienced criminals' defence options. Fortunately, many judges, magistrates, and juries see through such tactics, but often the outcome will be an investigation into the alleged police conduct. The effect of which is that the career of the officer(s) concerned will be put on hold while the matters are examined; or worse, an officer might be suspended from duty if there is an allegation of perjured evidence. As worryingly, some police officers giving evidence in court will be asked by defence lawyers whether they have been subject of a complaint, or whether they are currently under investigation as a result of a complaint. The officer will hopefully answer truthfully, but if indeed that is the case, much might then be made of the officers' alleged previous conduct and thus used to undermine the weight and credibility given to the evidence. There have been a number of instances where such tactics have been used, and where complaints have been fabricated against officers in advance of criminal trials, in order that this line can be taken to discredit an officer's evidence.

The role of the so-called corrupting criminals is a significant concern for those officers charged with investigating serious and organised crime and other criminal activity where the stakes are high and the potential criminal gain is significant. Such career criminals who suspect that they are attracting the attention of police will invariably deploy any feasible tactics to avoid arrest and subsequent prosecution. Lesser criminals might be paid for establishing contact with identified officers and then offering inducements to falsify or disregard evidence. Having done so, whether successfully or not, the matter can then be made subject of an official complaint against the officer, which can later be brought up in court if necessary. There are a number of variations to this particular tactic, all of which have the sole purpose of discrediting police evidence and police officers.

The solution to these underhand schemes lies in the hands of senior police officers, who must be aware of the vulnerability of their officers when tackling major crime and criminals. A range of anti-corruption measures can be introduced to ensure, as far as possible, that officers are protected from the attention of corrupting criminals and the misuse of the complaints system for criminal purposes. It will always be a difficult topic to raise with police officers, as the assumption will be that the officers will feel they are suspected of corrupt practice, which for the vast majority will be far from the truth. However, when the vulnerability of officers to corrupting criminals is exposed, most will be only too willing to embrace the procedures necessary to minimise their personal risk, and the risk to their investigations.

Of course it is tempting, when dealing with experienced criminals, to consider that any complaint they make about police is being made for some devious purpose. However, it is clear that they are as entitled to complain about police wrongdoing as any law abiding person. Assumptions must not be made on the basis of who is making the complaint; allegations must be examined and judged on the evidence.

One of the aggravating factors that frequently arise when allegations of police misconduct are made public in a very high profile way is the behaviour of individuals in powerful and influential positions, such as politicians, community leaders, and similar. It is not uncommon for alleged police misconduct that is considered sensational to be vigorously reported in the media. Such revelations are then often followed by a series of equally high profile calls for a '...most thorough investigation...', '...no stone must be left unturned...', '...police must be held to account...', and so on, from individuals who seek publicity by being seen to demonstrate their rigour. The problem is that such remarks, when made vigorously and publicly by high profile people, places enormous pressure on those conducting the investigation. Investigators will naturally feel that they have to ensure and then demonstrate that everything is being done that can be done, not only to search for the truth, but to demonstrate absolute thoroughness. Such pressure is generally unnecessary and should be resisted by those leading investigations in order to avoid over zealousness and the corresponding disproportionate use of powers. Confidence in the systems for exposing wrong doing should be sufficient, but if this is not present, then it is the systems that should be changed, not undue pressure applied to those responding.

The use of suspension from duty is a typical example of where the appropriate response to a high profile, or serious complaint has to be carefully considered. Obviously, when such a complaint is received, if officer(s) involved are promptly suspended from duty, a very clear signal is sent to both public and police that the matter is being taken most seriously and immediate action is being taken. However, the guidance on the use of suspension is quite clear and consideration must be given to factors including whether the continued presence of the officer at work might prejudice an investigation by risking loss of evidence or interference with witnesses. Also, whether the officer remaining at work will serve the public interest, having regard to the nature of the allegation. In this respect, it is always possible to move the officers(s) to tasks that do not involve contact with the public, thus avoiding the risk of any further allegations or repeat offending. In short, suspension is an option only in the most serious cases where the necessary conditions are met and which then has to be balanced against the traumatic effect that suspension will have on an officer, his family, and future working life. If suspension is considered to be the only satisfactory means of facilitating an investigation, it is customary to appoint a liaison officer to stay in touch with the suspended person and to provide a line of communication with the organisation. Regular reviews, at least weekly, must be undertaken to confirm that the decision to suspend remains appropriate and that circumstances have not altered to a point where the officer can be returned to work.

These and associated matters are vitally important to all those concerned; the complainant, the officers, witnesses, and others who are anxious about ensuring the best quality of police service delivery. It is essential, therefore, that such decisions are carefully considered.

It has been shown that an essential feature of policing by consent is a swift, efficient, and professionally competent complaint investigation system. Police forces invest a great deal of staff and other resources in ensuring this capability is available and the IOPC must do the same. At the time of writing, the Home Office has significantly increased the level of resources available to the IOPC, whilst at the same time reducing the budgets of territorial police forces. This move has predictably attracted a good deal of criticism from some police professionals, who argue that the increase should not be at the at the expense of the police professional standards departments and front line services. That said, as noted in Chapter Six, experienced investigators are not numerous and it will prove difficult to recruit individuals with the necessary attributes who would be attracted to such work. It would be unfortunate indeed, though, if poor quality investigators, poorly led, resulted in even slower and incomplete investigations. As in such events, neither complainant nor accused officer would be satisfied.

It does seem as though the workload of the IOPC has increased significantly, with investigations being undertaken into very protracted and, in some cases, historical events that can easily consume significant resources. As mentioned earlier, however, such pressures must not be allowed to result in investigations being unduly protracted, which certainly seems to have been a feature of many recent cases.

There are clearly further improvements that might be made to these systems that would speed matters along and provide more consistency of outcomes. Consideration might be given to establishing a public, standing police disciplinary tribunal, which would not only bring some consistency to punishments and sanctions for police wrongdoing, but also to the conduct of disciplinary proceedings and hearings generally. Such a solution could also have a positive effect by consistently and explicitly specifying behaviours and conduct that are absolutely unacceptable in policing and police officers. This could also have an equally positive influence on the public perception of police integrity, which has been shown to be vital to the concept of policing by consent and to the often much maligned police culture. There are of course difficulties to be overcome in relation to such a change, amongst which are the protection of some witness identities, the protection of intelligence sources, including informants, other data protection issues, the confidentiality of some police methods and capability, and of course matters relating to national security. It is, however, argued that the benefits would significantly outweigh these difficulties, which, given the will, could be overcome.

Since completing this chapter (2021) the issue of public confidence in policing and the police complaints system has become a much more serious problem as a result of string of high profile, serious crimes committed by serving officers. In some cases, these have arisen by officers using their professional position to facilitate crimes against their victims.

Thankfully such occurrences have been proportionally very few, but there is no doubting the extremely negative public reaction to confidence in police and policing. National and local politicians have also not been slow to call for tighter controls on professional practices, vetting and ethical standards.

Notwithstanding the earlier observations in this chapter that remain valid, there is no doubt that there is a pressing need to implement changes to the police complaints and disciplinary systems that will rectify this situation and restore a high level of public confidence, especially with regard to the recognition of serious and criminal allegations and the speed of following action.

Policing is too important to the maintenance of a high quality society to allow the individual rights of officers who seriously transgress the professional code of conduct to take precedence over the public common good and therefor by extension, undermine the concept of policing by consent.

Such a controversial change would clearly be contrary to established jurisprudential principles insofar as it is generally accepted that any person, including police officers, who are accused of any wrongdoing, are innocent until proved guilty.

However, it is argued that the current situation requires a fundamental change and it is proposed that this should be the implementation of a system of summary dismissal. When a serious complaint allegation about officers' misconduct is received by a police force through any route, whether apparently criminal or not, a swift scoping investigation as described in chapter six should be implemented by the receiving force, testing the allegation on the basis of the balance of probabilities, rather than the court test of beyond reasonable doubt. If the circumstances of the allegation appear to meet this test, the officer(s) concerned should be summarily dismissed by their own force. As opposed to being suspended on full pay and subjected to a lengthy investigation probably by the IOPC with little guarantee that the officer might return to duty if the evidence is insufficient for a prosecution, a situation that few would find satisfactory. It also seems that suspension on full pay provides a disincentive for any urgent investigative action which in turn introduces a number of avoidable difficulties, such as witness recollection and account variation.

Such a procedure would not be without implementation problems, but victims and witnesses have a perfectly reasonable expectation that when something criminal or anti-social is reported or they are involved in an operational issue, the police person with whom they are involved will be a person of the highest integrity. They must know they will be honest, true to their word, deal with issues expeditiously, not reveal confidentialities by gossip or through any internet social media platforms and deal with matters according to the professional code of conduct. Serious derogation of professional standards cannot be tolerated and such occurrences must be seen to be dealt with swiftly and effectively. Therefore, the public is entitled to know that the person dealing with their often sensitive issues, is an officer or other police person who themself is subject to the most rigorous professional standards.

The with-drawl of the right to be considered innocent until proved guilty would be a major change to police employment conditions, but no more so than the statutory removal of the right to strike that applies to police. Doubtless, the police staff associations would want to protect the rights of their members but they are also the least likely to want to protect wrongdoers. It may be that the concept of summary dismissal without necessarily implementing a full investigation could be introduced with some form of salary enhancement, in much the same way as removal of the right to strike was compensated in officers' salaries. There is no doubt that the introduction of such a procedure would enhance the status of police officers which would be seen as a positive outcome by the staff associations and avoid the assertion that officers were being treated in a disproportionally negative way. Of course, there would need to be a defined appeal procedure for a summary dismissal decision and a notice explaining the detail and procedure of such a process might be served on an officer upon leaving. However, the over-riding message to victims and the public is that the wider interest is most important and the police are not about protecting their own.

It would be important though to ensure that the scoping investigation of the allegation(s) referred to earlier was sufficiently thorough to acquire any relevant evidence that might be lost over time, such as digital data from relevant devices, physical witness accounts and of course offering the accused officer the opportunity to direct the investigation to material that might be discovered to refute the allegation. It would be important here to caution the officer that evidential material to be relied upon later, but not identified now could be inadmissible at any future appeal or criminal proceeding, such as alibi or explanation.

It is clear that if such a scheme were to be most effective then it would need to be administered by the accused officers' employing police force. Establishing a strong leadership approach and setting standards at the top to serious mis-conduct will send a very clear message to the organisation and drive the necessary culture and behaviour change. However, such a local and internal process might in turn create allegations and suspicions of conflicts of interests, or at worse favouritism. So, it would be necessary to give police forces the opportunity to refer cases where such situations might be suspected to another police force to conduct the scoping investigation and to make recommendations concerning dismissal. The emphasis here must be on speed of decision making and a transparency of both process and facts, without which the public cannot be reassured that robust professional standards exist.

The police code of conduct described earlier really needs to be refined and publicised in a persuasive and recurring way at every opportunity. A professional code of conduct must include ethical topics, quality and style of service delivery as well as specific subjects that address common issues of public concern, such as victim support, speed of response, and transparency coupled with the necessity for the confidentiality of some information and individuals' identity. Such a process would bring to public attention the standards to which police officers operate and the way they are individually held accountable for compliance with the code, ensuring the survival of policing by consent with the associated public confidence.

10.

Making Transitions

Police organisations must be agile

In the context of the suggestions and propositions advanced here, it is important to discuss the processes and outcomes of organisational change, and the effects of change on the workplace and working protocols for all employees, in order to create agile police organisations that are responsive to external inputs.

In the past, conservative thinking in police organisations has resulted in a resistance to changes in police practices, even where inefficiencies are apparent. Given that now this review of some policing issues has made a number of suggestions for significant changes to be made to police practice and policy, it seems reasonable to offer some further suggestions as to how to tackle the issue of change management in policing and how to bring about lasting improvements.

The terms 'leadership' and 'management' are used somewhat interchangeably here, which of course is hardly precise. Suffice to say that in terms of leading and managing change, there are essentially three aspects of the task, communication, planning, and organising, by which it is meant allocating tasks with clear outcomes to named individuals; objective setting.

An additional problem is that there seems to be an absence of any unifying theory of change management, which is probably due to the complexity and diversity of the factors that are potentially relevant to organisational change processes. For instance, factors as diverse as individual psychological phenomena through to macro-economic and political influences, with much in between, may all have a bearing on the propensity and willingness to change and the speed at which it is achievable.

It is apparent that the effects and consequences of organisational change are often found to have an impact far beyond the immediate issue that creates the need for change. For instance, apparently minor changes to shift work patterns and rotas can have profound consequences for those undertaking their duties during what are normally considered to be anti-social hours. Police officers, medical staff, train drivers, commercial pilots, and others working variable shift patterns will all be acutely aware of such difficulties, many of whom have raised issues arising from such changes in very high profile ways. The personal impact of variable shift work patterns on health, sleep, appetite, lifestyle, and concentration are now very well known.

A dilemma often considered by individuals leading change in a large organisation is whether to make changes incrementally and observe success before moving on, or whether to make simultaneous changes across a broad scope. In order to more accurately understand the effect of the combination of factors at work during processes of change, and in particular with regard to police organisations, it is necessary to have an integrated, or holistic approach to changes. This means identifying all the relevant parts of the system that will be affected by the change(s) and having a plan for each. It is, however, clear that by concentrating on limited change process factors, such as psychosocial matters, structures, operating procedures, etc. then it is probable that unforeseen consequences will appear that will limit the anticipated benefits of the changes. It is likely to be the combination of such change factors that cause the dysfunctional affects, as well as unforeseen external influences that are beyond the control of change leaders and managers. Therefore, the potentially more successful way of introducing significant changes to working practices is to tackle the full scope of the required changes simultaneously.

The concept of the degree of *openness* of police organisations and systems is generally well understood. It can be seen that, as the police became more engaged with the communities they serve and more aware of local policing problems and priorities, so the police systems become progressively more *open*. The degree of *openness* is characterised by a greater quantity of information being exchanged between police and public, facilitated by more numerous channels and means for information exchange. This concept is in contrast to a more *closed* organisation, or system, which shares little information with its environment, thus potentially being more isolated and more resistant to change.

The problem at present is that a combination of factors has prevented police forces from continuing to become more open and indeed driven towards a more closed and reactive style of policing. Resource reductions are an obvious factor in this process, whether brought about by finance policy, increasing demands, or policy alterations, which create additional burdens, leading to less time for preventive measures. Simply, the greater the public demand for reactive police services, the less time is available for pro-active community engagement. A problem encountered by many other public services!

In the past it was found to be necessary for the police to make determined and continuing efforts to stimulate additional channels of communication with the public so that this 'greater openness' would follow. Neighbourhood watch schemes were set up, approaches were made to residents' groups, social clubs, other societies, and community based initiatives were encouraged by the police in order to engage with them for the purpose of aiming at crime prevention and improving quality of life. So, external communication was not seen as something that was inherently good in itself, but as a means of stimulating the police organisation to respond to public needs. It now seems that this process has stalled, with the result being that policing has become a much more reactive service with little crime and disorder preventive activities taking place. The necessity of increasing external communication, and thus *openness*, is, however, fundamental if the police expect the public to support them and to give life to and maintain the philosophy of 'policing by consent'. It is unrealistic to expect public support if the public don't know what the police are doing; how can someone contribute to an outcome if they don't know what it is?

Experience with Neighbourhood Policing teams across the country demonstrated that, as this *openness* increased, so too would the volume of information passing between the police and the public. This in turn would help to determine police priorities in terms of when, where, and at which problems police resources would be directed. However, the significant reduction in the number and size of these Neighbourhood Policing teams has, in many cases, deprived police forces of the means by which they gain much information, as well as the means of delivering solutions. These limitations apply equally to the whole range of police services, from vital community intelligence concerning preparation for acts of terrorism to quality of life issues affecting the day-to-day experiences of communities. It might be readily appreciated, however, that this greater exchange and flow of information would in fact create a more *open* organisation that would be more susceptible to unplanned changes from influences that are outside the organisations control. This inevitably leads to the proposition that more *open* organisations will change more frequently than those that possess more *closed* characteristics. It might further be proposed that a good deal of such change will be unplanned, rather than change as a controlled process with a defined purpose and outcome.

In order to manage the change processes with a little more certainty, an overall model of change can be proposed to aid analysis of both planned and unplanned change. The model has three stages. Firstly to identify the *origins* of the change, secondly to identify the *target* for the change, and thirdly to select the method of *implementation*.

Respecting the *origin* of change; does the impetus come from outside the organisation or within, or a combination of both? For example, a drive for a more participative management style might be a feature of 'management fashion', the origin of which might arise from society itself and the expectations of younger people entering the workplace, or forced by government through new laws. The impetus might, however, arise from a community, or a sub-set of a community, such as places of entertainment, shops, and residents, etc. who have ambitions to be more involved in a public service management process. Whatever the origin of the impetus, the rigorous identification of the source of the potential change might seem trivial, but it is in fact essential. It will identify the places and procedures within an organisation that are likely to be at the forefront of the changes; in other words, the *target* of the change, and it will facilitate the development of measures that will enable success or otherwise to be assessed.

This concept of a *target* of change is the second element of the proposed model. The notion is that the actual parts of an organisation that are likely to experience the effect of the change are clearly identified. The change might be targeted at operating procedures and systems. In other words, how things are done and work carried out. However, the target(s) might include structures, divisions of labour, accountability relationships, rules, etc. as well as less tangible features of organisations, such as culture, psycho-social factors, and other human phenomena.

The third element of the model is the selected method of implementation, which should of course be decided upon in the light of knowledge from stages one and two. Changes might be made suddenly, gradually over time, in phases, or after pilot schemes and experiments. A good deal of careful consideration here will determine the extent to which a change can be effective, given the method of implementation. A slow and progressive change programme might be less challenging and more comfortable for those affected, but with the accompanying risk that the change target will slip back to the previous state if the process is too gradual. An obvious example here would be the changes necessary to evidential disclosure procedures (Chapter Six). Here police, the Crown Prosecution Service, the courts, and criminal lawyers all need to be familiar with requirements and be satisfied that the rules are practicable, as well as providing the necessary safeguards for victims, witnesses, and suspects. Probably not something to be rushed. Conversely, a sudden change on, say, a given date might produce confusion and inefficiencies in the short term, but actually achieve a greater impact in the fullness of time, such as a new piece of procedural or proscriptive legislation. There are clearly a variety of implementation techniques in between these two extremes and it is a matter for the change managers and leaders to determine which is best suited to their particular situation, having regard to the planned and unplanned aspects of the changes to be implemented.

As mentioned previously, the very firmly entrenched culture amongst many police officers and, to some extent, police staff has been created and sustained by adherence to the operational policies and practices that have been seen as necessary and successful in the past and amount to a common belief '...that is the way things are done here...'. Many such procedures are, of course, based on legal requirements (rules of evidence, victim/witness care, and investigative procedures, amongst others). Other external effects over which the police have very limited influence are also significant, such as sentencing policies, parenting skills, (mis)use of social media, and other social trends. But it is likely that the apparent reluctance of police organisations to quickly embrace change has its origins in these cultural and procedural practices, which extends into police management policies. It might be argued that it is important for the police to resist some external change drivers that are potentially damaging to society, but it may also be argued that it is important for the police to reflect a changing society and follow social trends. These are clearly matters for wide consultation and, in some cases, government guidance; they are most definitely not to be ignored.

In order to overcome staff resistance to change, which as described is a particularly robust feature of police culture, there is the need for effective internal communication. It is suggested that if major changes are proposed to working or employment practices, then a dedicated and focused internal communications programme is necessary. Obvious examples of such effective communication are the type and extent of such initiatives directed at staff within merged organisations, where differing cultures are apparent, or where new maintenance or operating procedures are necessary.

Such police internal communication should include regular, persuasive demonstrations of the positive features of the change(s), by describing why the changes are necessary, and the available options, with the advantages and benefits to those involved. There should be a presentation of a rational analysis of the inappropriateness of the former situation or policy, associated with the method of achievement for the required changes and the internal rewards policy. So advancement, specialisation, training opportunities, and other tangible inducements are strongly associated with achievement of, and compliance with, the required changes. Of course, such internal communication needs to be positive and encouraging, but also outlining negative situations to be avoided.

The opportunities available through effective external communication can also be harnessed as a powerful means of achieving positive staff attitudes and tackling potential change resistance. Advice from media professionals will be invaluable here, especially in respect of defining and rehearsing the key messages to deliver. The outcome has the potential to develop opinions of influential people that are broadly supportive of the proposed changes, such as friends and family of staff and other public opinion formers at all levels. A further opportunity may be created as awareness of previously unmentioned negative arguments arise, which might then be taken into account.

Very often, and despite effective internal and external communications, individuals will resist change for a range of personal reasons that are not necessarily associated with the strong police culture. Uncertainty is a typical problem that arises from simply not knowing in sufficient detail what is required in the new order of things. It may be that the new situation is inherently uncertain, but it is more likely that uncertainty will be apparent if internal communication has been weak or confusing. Confusion in itself is often sufficient to prevent someone from accepting change and usually occurs as a result of poorly designed and delivered internal communication. Some individuals are, of course, more confident than others and will be more willing to embrace change if they can see the value of it. So, as in any organisation, it is important for police leaders to be attuned to the needs of their staff and quick to support those lacking confidence. Many people do, however, resist change to their working practices and are unable to reconcile any change due to their personal high levels of anxiety, leading to stress and fear. This might be perfectly rational to such staff if job losses seem to be in prospect, but even if the required changes necessitate a complete change of role, such a prospect can seem very frightening to some and they are unlikely to be able to embrace what is required. This may not be a deliberate awkwardness, or obstruction, but simply a fear of the unknown. Here again, police leaders should be sensitive to these signals and devote time to supplement the formal communications by encouraging understanding of the reasons for change.

In order to achieve this outcome in policing systems, which are inherently complex, it is unlikely that all the skills required to achieve lasting change will be available in one or a few officers and members of staff. Rather, the necessary complimentary skills and experience should be incorporated in a 'change team', or 'task force' with the responsibility and authority to carry forward the change programme. Such a group should report directly to a member of the chief officer team and not be a part of the existing line management structure.

It is tempting to assume that resistance to change is always a negative phenomenon, although it is frequently perceived in that way. Organisations, whether public service or private sector, have a need to pursue multiple objectives for survival, and amongst these, there is likely to be a need for some stability, balanced with need to adapt or change. Clearly, the type and purpose of an organisation will, to a large extent, determine this balance. A business in the competitive mobile phone industry, for instance, will clearly experience and indeed encourage change and innovation. In contrast to, say, a government department that might see itself as providing some stability in the face of political changes.

Police organisations, especially those operating within large, urban conurbations, carry out their functions in extremely turbulent environments, where both public and political opinions can fluctuate rapidly and widely. To correspondingly react to all such fluctuations would severely curtail the ability of the police to strategically tackle crime and the other demands on their services. Similarly, in police organisations where operational experience is a valued attribute, too much disruptive change, resulting in a high staff turnover or other diversion of expertise, would not be viewed in a positive light. In such circumstances, resistance to externally stimulated change would, to some extent, amount to a corporate asset, rather than a constraint. Whereas in an organisation that was dependent upon a creative reaction to its operating environment, the balance would favour adaptive staff who are less inclined to exhibit values and behaviour associated with the established norm.

A time plan is essential, which must describe the anticipated progress of the proposed changes and the combination of non-negotiable and participative changes foreseen. Everyone must be clear about those aspects of the current situation that can be changed and directed towards the vision with staff involvement, in contrast to those aspects of the changes that will be made with or without the active collaboration of the workforce: in other words, imposed changes. An example here would be the implementation of new equipment that cannot be quickly altered. The organisations' requirement would be that the new equipment will be adopted, but there may be a possibility for adaptation in the future. Such an example does, however, pose the question as to why there wasn't productive engagement with user staff before procurement of new equipment?

There is no doubting that change management is one of the most demanding managerial functions, which seems to be increasing in both difficulty and pace. Major events, many of which are largely outside the control or influence of police leaders, appear to be becoming more common, imposing an increasing need for significant changes to police organisations. Issues such as the governmental financial austerity, political swings towards greater populism, the decision of the UK to leave the EU, the apparently numerous, high profile complaints of predatory sexual behaviour allegedly committed by some celebrities, and the Supreme Court decision (2018) to require police to investigate all serial and serious crime allegations in defence of victims' human rights, all have a bearing on how the police policies direct operational effectiveness. Similarly, the so-called county lines drug dealing networks and the ever increasing use of the internet for fraud, immigration, and grooming crimes all present new challenges for police. Such events, and likely many other external disruptions, impose a clear need for police operational and support service policies to be reviewed with the consequent need for change in many cases. This in turn will significantly raise the need for heightened change leadership and management skills in policing organisations, if major deterioration in operational performance and public confidence are to be avoided.

11.

In a nutshell

Summary, Conclusions, and Suggestions

Resources, and in particular staffing levels, are a problem. Twenty thousand less police officers since 2010 will inevitably lead to adjustments as to how officers allocate their time, and the consequences of diminished front line policing needs to be considered. There is clearly a limit to the scope of efficiency improvements that can be made and eventually service levels will become adversely affected. Recent history shows that the first activities to fall away in such circumstances are crime and public disorder prevention tactics, followed by reassurance and victim support measures.

The introduction of policies that are more time consuming, albeit necessary, have further eroded any remaining discretionary time. For instance, historic investigations, unquestioning acceptance of victim allegations in sexual offences, fraud, disclosure issues arising from computers, other data devices, and internet connectivity. There are more, but the point is established that police time consequences need to be considered and not ignored when policy and practice changes are made.

It has been repeatedly shown how important it is to reduce the accelerating trend towards a more reactive style of policing and return to patrol and investigation strategies that incorporate preventive features. Without such a change, response demands will continue to rise ahead of the ability and capacity of police to respond. Not a dis-similar situation to that observed in some other major public sector services (NHS, ambulances, prison and probation; the list could go on!). Such a police demand trend is not only economically damaging to the public, but also has a significant negative impact on quality of life issues. In a variety of contexts, however, it has been demonstrated that it is police response services that the public value most highly. But there needs to be sufficient time remaining in officers' shifts for them to engage in preventive tactics to apply amelioration to this trend. In effect, this means that shift patterns and patrol deployments need to more closely follow demand profiles. It is a very straightforward analysis to understand, on a routine basis, where and when public demands are at their most frequent and to deploy officers accordingly. Clearly, when successful, the demand profile will alter and it will be necessary to alter deployments to reflect these changes. Thus the solution to this demand-led situation becomes more complicated, emphasising the need for more sophisticated measurement methods.

Similarly, the speed of response is important. Not necessarily setting targets in this respect, but a prompt reaction to a call for assistance is an effective way of having early engagement with a problem, often before it becomes critical, but also securing public help in the future. A failure to respond to victims' circumstances is not going to encourage confidence and the motivation to assist police in the future.

The speed of investigations is also important, not only to victims and witnesses, but for successful identification and recovery of evidence. Dilatory investigations that are not adequately resourced and properly supervised, with other delays such as slow forensic analysis, are invariably unsuccessful. As noted in Chapter Six, various creative schemes to screen out those cases that do not show the early characteristics of being successful have not provided the anticipated benefits to either police or victims. A successful strategy would be to test the allegation(s) and then pursue investigations until it becomes apparent that a solution will not be readily found, or where, with more time, a suspect will be identified with the availability of adequate evidence to support a prosecution. This implies sufficient trained investigators to meet demands.

A recent example of fraud victims being led to believe their case will be investigated, only to later discover that no action has been taken, does not inspire public confidence in the police, the willingness to report fraud in the future, or comfort in personal financial security. There is absolutely no good reason, though, why a good deal of work associated with many investigations could not be undertaken by officers working from home, given suitably secure technology and access to corporate databases. Clearly, this would not be appropriate in many cases, but encouraging such a policy could bring some significant improvements to case performance, as well as to officers and to officer retention.

Such a development could also yield benefits in other areas, such as recruitment. It should be appreciated that many people do not want to follow a career path spanning thirty or so years, but rather want to enjoy a variety of employments and experiences at appropriate times in their life. The investigation of internet facilitated fraud cases is an obvious example of where specialist skills and knowledge from the commercial sector might be applied to a growing problem. Such a policy could also facilitate the attraction of individuals with diverse skills and the retention of both men and women who prefer family friendly working conditions. It is appreciated that security will always be critical and it is clear that any breaches of security, in the form of data loss or corruption, unauthorised access to files, or any other interference, would seriously compromise a home working policy. These problems, however, are more easily solved than the compounded and aggravated injury to victims brought about by slow investigations, as well as the corresponding reputational damage to police.

Changes of this type would necessitate a major overhaul of police remuneration. The current national pay scales, largely linked to rank, time serving, and pension conditions, with some minor regional variations, are simply not fit for purpose in the twenty-first century. Flexible salary packages allowing for differing working times and conditions linked to skills, experience, and specialist knowledge are necessary to attract capable, well-motivated people to the stimulating work of policing. In combination with continuing recruitment policies to fully replace the single point of entry system, such changes will meet the police staffing needs for the foreseeable future. It is likely, however, that any proposals to change current remuneration systems would be met with opposition from police staff associations, who would doubtless see local agreements as an erosion of their national negotiating power.

Closely linked to the speed of investigations is the speed of the criminal justice system (CJS). As the title implies, it is a 'system' in that each element, the police, the Crown Prosecution Service, the Courts, and the Prison and Probation services, are dependent upon each other for collective success, which includes prompt outcomes for all concerned, with successful convictions for police and prosecutors. However, it is too easy for elements of the CJS to work in isolation, assuming that due process takes the time it takes, regardless of the effect on the other parts of the system, and of course it takes only one dilatory performing element for the whole system to slow down. The consequence of a sluggish CJS is that a culture of tolerance to a lack of urgency develops. The norm then becomes that unless sufficient time is expended, and a thorough consideration of the matter in hand hasn't been made (Not dis-similar to being seen working late at a desk without necessarily achieving anything).

It is unfortunate that the police have not yet been able to anything like fully exploit the potential benefits of much technological innovation. Applications such as data networks for neighbourhood policing teams, linked to corporate databases for intelligence purposes, access via portable devices, portable analysis equipment for phones and data tablets are just a few of the areas that could benefit in both efficiency and effectiveness. It is apparent, however. that officers delivering front line services are not fully aware of the technological solutions that could contribute to their work. The people who do have access to such developmental initiatives and the budgets are very often risk averse, especially in relation to resource use; failure being seen as a negative outcome.

In many police forces, this is a consequence of time served structures, where the operational delivery elements of the organisation are separate from the support service functions; it might cynically be commented that the role of the latter is to constrain the former. However, the issue of organisational structures has and will in the future consume a great deal of time and energy. The conflict between local accountability and regional or national models will also generate much debate. It is clear, however, that changes are becoming increasingly necessary. It is an established fact that the structure of an organisation will shape the style of service delivery. That being the case, and given the public's preference for local response services, adequately resourced neighbourhood policing teams should provide the basic structural building block. A communications and data network, linked to specialist services at a regional level, could group these teams together. The teams do not need to be of a regular size, but rather comprising a number of officers and staff appropriate to the area being policed. The important factor is to maintain the team numbers and not allow abstractions to make the team dysfunctional. Geographically larger areas of a lower population having proportionally bigger teams, with longer travelling distances, may need a different mix of staff and skills than for urban centres of population with geographically smaller areas to cover. Similarly, team leaders do not need to be of equivalent rank or grade, which would depend on the nature of the area being policed; more challenging environments requiring more experienced leaders than others.

This model, built on neighbourhood policing teams, implies the appointment of a regional head of operations who's role would be to co-ordinate operational services, oversee major investigations, and maximise the use and benefit of supplementary and specialist resources.

In fact, a very similar role to that undertaken by an assistant chief constable (operations) within the current structure, but encompassing a much larger and populous area. Such regional units could be clustered and administered by a chief constable, who would also have responsibility for the cluster's back office and support functions, such as finance, facilities management, people, and so on, recognising the importance of regional, cultural identities (Chapter Three).

Such a model would reduce the current number of police headquarters and chief constables from forty-three to just a handful. The public would benefit from local accountability through the neighbourhood policing teams, with their associated consultative processes, and operational efficiency would be improved by the availability of specialist support at a regional level (Chapter Three). As far as external accountability is concerned, clearly the role of Police and Crime Commissioners would need to change with the consequential cost savings and separation from direct political influence. Chief Constables might be appointed and held to public account by a small committee, comprising of local authority and Home Office representatives, with an input from other parts of the criminal justice system and interest groups, such as victim support, social services, etc. thus making the body responsible for performance across the police and prosecution functions (Chapter Four). Indeed, such a group would not be very dissimilar in make-up and functioning to the now defunct police community consultative groups.

The inclusion of vetted, non-execute directors at this level would improve openness and diversity. It is not necessary for such committees to be large and expensive to administer. For instance, not all local authorities need to have a representative present, this could be organised on a rotational basis. It would seem that a maximum of twenty delegates would be an efficient size, meeting perhaps twelve times per year. Anything more weighty than this would create an unnecessary bureaucracy, which will eventually seek greater management influence over police operations and is exactly the situation the proposed model seeks to avoid; the strategy being to make senior police officers responsible and accountable for service delivery as they are eminently qualified to do.

Some of the changes proposed in the preceding chapters may seem radical and difficult to achieve, but it should be appreciated that, with a few exceptions, the structures and operational procedures of policing are not vastly changed since the end of World War Two. Indeed, some might argue that matters have deteriorated since then, so time now to venture 'Deep Into the Blue'.

James Hart is a retired Commissioner of Police for the City of London.
He is a successful architect of change in Policing.
'Neighbourhood Policing'.
He is currently a consultant in safety and security issues.